Ano

Chloralamid Schering:

The new hypnotic discovered by Dr. J. von Mering, of Strassburg. Fourth

Edition

Anonymous

Chloralamid Schering:
The new hypnotic discovered by Dr. J. von Mering, of Strassburg. Fourth Edition

ISBN/EAN: 9783337818135

Printed in Europe, USA, Canada, Australia, Japan

Cover: Foto ©ninafisch / pixelio.de

More available books at **www.hansebooks.com**

SCHERING.

THE NEW HYPNOTIC.

DISCOVERED BY
DR. J. VON MERING, OF STRASSBURG.

PATENTED AND MANUFACTURED BY

Chemische Fabrik auf Actien,

vormals E. Schering),

BERLIN.

FOURTH REVISED EDITION.

PUBLISHED BY
LEHN & FINK,
SOLE AGENTS AND LICENSEES FOR AMERICA,
New York, October, 1892.

CONTENTS.

INTRODUCTORY.

CHLORALAMID-Schering is now the approved new hypnotic.

A little over a year ago this product was introduced to the medical profession of this country, coming with the excellent recommendations of its discoverer, Dr. J. von MERING, and of such clinical authorities as Drs. HAGEN and HUEFLER of Erlangen, REICHMANN of Giessen, HAGEMANN and STRAUSS of Bonn, KNY of Strassburg, ALT of Halle o. S., Prof. S. RABOW of Lausanne-Cery, and PEIPER of Greifswalde, by whom preliminary tests had been made, and on whose united favorable reports the new hypnotic found a ready welcome. Since then the action of CHLORALAMID has been jealously scrutinized and widely and carefully tested by friendly, impartial and inimical investigators, and the concensus of opinions thus gathered is to-day an unqualified endorsement of the general value, the therapeutical efficiency and physiological harmlessness, and of the safety, reliability and superior effect of CHLORALAMID as a hypnotic.

In the following pages are presented the contributions of eminent practitioners: impartial, critical, and accurate reporters, whose labors in this work gain in value because entirely gratuitous and unsolicited, and prompted only by their interest in new therapeutics and the desire to prove the merits of the remedy.

It is unnecessary to refer in detail to the following pages, or to recapitulate the views and facts presented. An intelligent and careful perusal and study of all the contents will suffice to impart full and accurate information concerning CHLORALAMID, and will in our opinion convince all practitioners—the favorably disposed and the skeptical—that where a hypnotic is desirable in their practices, they can serve their patients best by administering CHLORALAMID by one or the other of the approved methods presented herein.

CHLORALAMID—Schering.

By Chas. H. Steele, A.M., M.D.,

Professor of Materia Medica and Therapeutics, Cooper Medical College.

From *Pacific Medical Journal*.

Chloralamid is properly a chloralformamid, or formidate of chloral, with the formula $CCL_3CH \begin{cases} OH \\ NHCHO. \end{cases}$

It is chemically a union of chloral anhydride (CCl_3CHO) with formamide ($CHO.NH_2$).

Prof. J. von Mering was its discoverer and E. Schering, of Berlin, is its exclusive manufacturer. It occurs in the form of colorless, very faintly but not unpleasantly bitter, non-caustic, crystals, melting at 239° F., and is soluble in from nine to fourteen parts of cold and less of warm water, in one part of absolute, and one and a half parts of ninety-six per cent. alcohol. To understand its time of action it is well to remember that it requires five hours to dissolve twenty grains in two ounces of water, and only fifteen minutes when the menstruum is one dram of rectified spirit. No precipitation occurs on adding the alcoholic solution to water.

TESTS.

Upon heating chloralamid to its melting point, 239° F., chloral is liberated and may be tested separately. Heated with a solution of potassa it emits odors of chloroform and ammonia. A few grains in a solution of four drops of ninety per cent. carbolic acid added to one-half ounce of strong sulphuric acid, gradually heated to boiling, gives rise to a bright-red color and a strong odor of chlorine. With the same test phenacetin produces a dark purplish-brown mixture with a strong acetous odor, and with sulphonal, a bright green, changing to dark green upon the further addition of strong sulphurous acid.   Fehling's and Pavy's solutions are not affected by chloralamid.

INCOMPATIBLES.

The drug is rapidly decomposed by water heated above 140° F. and by caustic alkalies, and slowly by alkaline carbonates.

ADMINISTRATION.

The dose varies from fifteen to sixty grains, while the majority of experimenters rely upon a single dose of thirty grains and rarely find forty-five grains necessary.   A few consider this last dose as the limit of safety.   A child of eleven years of age was given seven grains, and another four and a half years old, five and ten grains.   In any case it is better, especially with new drugs, to commence with the smallest dose and increase cautiously. To secure the best results the drug should be administered from one to one and one-half hours before bed-time.   It may be prescribed in powders, alone or triturated with oleosacchara fœniculi, in capsules, wafers, or dissolved in wine or brandy, to which water may be added as desired.   Some difficulty will be experienced in taking the powder in water, tea or milk, as advised by a few, on account of its slow solution and tendency to adhere to the sides of the vessel.   It is better to wash down the powder with a draught of milk, weak tea or water.   An advised prescription is:

R Chloralamid .... gr. xiv.
    Acidi Hydrochlorici Diluti .... gtt. vi.
    Syrupi Rubi Idæi .... ℥ ii.
    Aquæ q. s. ad...................... ℥   ii.
       Sig. To be taken in one or two doses.

As an enema, in which form it is unirritating and slow in action, we may use:

R Chloralamid...................... gr. xiv.
    Acidi Hydrochlorici Diluti .... gtt. iii.
    Alcohol .... min. xx.
    Aquæ............................. ℥   iii.

So administered it is considered by a few to be most reliable in its action.

However used it must be remembered that its solution is not to be heated.

PHYSIOLOGICAL ACTION.

Locally, chloralamid has been found to be absolutely free from irritation, and even where a ten per cent. solution has been applied to the delicate conjunctiva. Internally, no effect has yet been discovered upon digestion and circulation, except in relation to the vaso motor centre. Here we have a trivial difference in opinion. A single authority (LANGGAARD)—a possible pessimist, for he also makes the same statement regarding the respiratory centre—affirms that blood pressure is lowered through depression of the vaso motor apparatus. REICHMANN admits that this is slightly so, but von MERING, ZUNTZ, Prof. LEECH of Guy's Hospital, GEO. P. COPE of Dublin and many others deny this action, while RABOW, of Lausanne, goes still further and states that the formamide, liberated from the chloral, stimulates the vaso motor centre in the medulla and raises blood pressure.

Chloralamid has the property of inducing an apparently natural sleep, commencing in from one-half to three hours and lasting from six to ten hours. The usual interval between the administration of the dose and the advent of sleep is from one to two hours, but this depends so greatly upon the slow solubility of the drug in the watery fluids of the stomach that it is possible that absorption may not be completed or sleep commence until the morning after the evening dose. This delay might be obviated by employing an alcoholic solution. In some cases the sleep is interrupted and even many failures are reported. However, all this depends upon the dose administered, forty-five grains—equalling thirty grains of chloral hydrate—being considered necessary to insure certainty. The frequency of the failures may be estimated from the fact that Dr. COPE reports only four per cent., Dr. WILLIAMS six and one-half per cent. of all cases, and Prof. LEECH no failures in nineteen patients. Some consider the sleep to be deeper than that obtained with chloral.

To what this hypnotic action is to be attributed is, as yet, only a matter of conjecture. Dr. EUGEN KNY supposes that, in the alkaline blood, chloral is gradually liberated, and he partially bases this opinion upon the presence of uro-chloralic acid in the urine. It would seem, however, that more depression would have been discovered if such were the case. The only depression positively established was that of reflex action in frogs after injecting one-third to one-half of a grain.

INCIDENTAL EFFECTS.

While no unpleasant after-effects were noticed by many authorities, no disturbance of the heart, respiration, temperature, kidneys, digestion, or appetite (but rather improvement of appetite, according to Dr. D. R. Paterson), a few have occasionally found slight headache upon awakening, alone or with lassitude, and a desire to sleep during the next morning or entire day. Among the other unusual effects are thus arranged in order, commencing with those most frequently reported: slight or severe vertigo, thirst, nausea, dryness of the mouth, loss of appetite, slight delirium, vomiting, cardiac weakness, rapid and feeble pulse and restlessness which necessitated forcible restraint. The more severe symptoms appeared after large doses, over thirty grains, and were not consecutive or persistent as is the case with sulfonal. Patients do not seem to become accustomed to its use, nor is there evidence that the drug is cumulative in action.

One hour after a dose of sixty grains, there have, in two instances, appeared vertigo, intoxication, volubility, inco-ordination, occipital headache, nausea, and either no change or slight increase in the pulse rate. These symptoms were at their height in about three hours after administering the dose, while slight vertigo and cephalalgia persisted during the second day.

These incidental effects seem to be very rarely exhibited, even after the largest therapeutic doses, and are proportionally not more frequent than with chloral or morphine.

THERAPEUTICS.

Chloralamid is successfully employed in conquering insomnia, and particularly that form denominated simple or ideopathic insomnia, not due to excitement or severe pain. It is, furthermore, possible for the wakeful patient to enjoy several nights of natural sleep after a single dose. The best results occur when the drug is used in insomnia due to nervousness, neurasthenia, hysteria, "spinal disease" or old age; next best when the causes are chronic alcoholism, alcohol excess, cardiac and bronchial asthma, pleuritis, phthisis, pericarditis, arterial sclerosis, organic heart disease, typhoid fever, gastritis, subacute nephritis, ascites, diabetes, mellitus and in the morphine habit. It is less effective when wake-fulness is due to tabes dorsalis, neuralgia, progressive paralysis, the excitement of insanity, cerebral softening with delirium, me-lancholia, chronic mania and acute mania. In these conditions, doses of from thirty to sixty grains are required, providing such doses are tolerated.

The drug is useless when the insomnia results from paralytic dementia, maniacal excitement or hallucinations, severe neuralgia or other pain, violent cough, distressing headache, delirium of ce-rebral apoplexy and from delirium tremens.

Even pain, when not acute, is often relieved, and the large doses necessitated are, by many patients, preferred to morphine. Chloralamid, in doses of from twenty to sixty grains, has checked the pains of thoracic aneurism, carcinoma of the stomach and liver, sarcoma of a rib, erysipelas, rheumatic fever, floating kid-ney, neuralgia, gallstone, varicose ulcer and alcoholic neurisis.

In chorea, a boy of eleven years of age was cured in five days by fifteen grains of the drug three times daily, and in like manner, a girl, after receiving no benefit from other forms of treatment, was afforded relief in eight days.

When administered in phthisis it was found that the trouble-some night sweats disappeared.

CHLORALAMID.

A Study of the Medicinal Value of this Hypnotic.

By JOHN V. SHOEMAKER, A.M., M.D.

Professor of Materia Medica, Pharmacology, Therapeutics, and Clinical Medicine, and Clinical Professor of Diseases of the Skin in the Medico-Chirurgical College of Philadelphia, etc.

Pharmacology.—Chloralamid, known also as chloralformamid or formidate of chloral, one of the recently introduced hypnotics, was first prepared by Prof. VON MERING, of Strassburg, and its manufacture upon a commercial scale has been entrusted to the great chemical house of SCHERING, in Berlin. Chloralamid is com-posed of two parts of chloral anhydride with one part of formamid. From a commercial point of view it possesses the advantage of cheapness, which cannot be overlooked.

This substance comes in the form of white granular crystals, which melt at 230° F. and dissolve slowly in about twenty parts of cold water, in one part of absolute alcohol, and in one and a half parts of 96 per cent. alcohol. The alcoholic solution is not precipitated by the addition of water. Although its solubility is increased in warm water, yet this fact is scarcely of practical advantage, or at least the temperature must be carefully observed, since chloralamid is destroyed when the mercury ascends above 140° F. It is decomposed by caustic alkalies and alkaline carbonates, which are consequently chemically incompatible with chloralamid. Chloral is set free when chloralamid is heated to its melting point. A good test for chloralamid is the addition of a few grains to a solution of four drops of ninety per cent. carbolic acid, and gradually heating the mixture to the boiling point with a half ounce of strong sulphuric acid, when a bright red color and a strong odor of chlorine appear.

Chloralamid is administered in doses ranging from 15 to 60 grains. In most cases in which it has been used 30 grains have been found sufficient. By some it has been given in the form of powder enclosed in capsules or cachets, but a better plan is to dissolve it in a portion of wine, whiskey or brandy. In order to obtain its therapeutical effects chloralamid should be exhibited a half hour before bed-time. It has been serviceably administered also in the form of an enema.

Physiological Action.—Chloralamid is devoid of local irritant properties, and a ten per cent. solution has been found entirely innocuous to the conjunctiva. It has but little taste, being but slightly bitterish, and is almost completely disguised by the liquor in which it is dissolved. Little or no deleterious influence is exerted by this drug upon the appetite or digestion. Dr. W. V. WHITMORE, of Los Angeles, Cal., found it to cause digestive disturbances in only one per cent. of the cases in which it was used, and it has occasionally produced vomiting. On the other hand a case is mentioned by Dr. D. R. PATERSON, in which the appetite improved while chloralamid was being taken, and UMPFENBACH remarks that in every instance it was well borne when taken for months at a time, and that the bodily weight never decreased during the treatment. Chloralamid is without action upon the bowels or kidneys. Most observers agree in the statement that no marked effect is produced either upon the respiration or circulation in the course of physiological or clinical experiments. Dr. George P. Cope * writes that in five cases—one of pneumonia, one of phthisis, one of cardiac disease, and two of insomnia—he obtained sphygmographic tracings before and after its administration, and the blood pressure was not lowered in any of them, while the respiration and temperature remained the same. The testimony of Dr. D. R. Paterson † is to the same effect. In eleven cases in which chloralamid was administered Dr. E. Reichmann, of Prof. Riegel's Clinic in Giessen, ‡ detected no depressant effect upon the circulation from two to four gramme doses. Sphygmographic tracings were made in these cases, and when measured with a V. Basch sphygmomanometer no considerable fluctuation in the pressure of the blood was noticed. Dr. Eugen Kny, of the clinic for mental diseases at the University of Strassburg, found that after internal administration or intravenous injection of chloralamid the blood pressure was not disturbed beyond the limit within which it may vary in a perfectly natural sleep. The heart continued to beat vigorously, and the blood pressure remained nearly at its normal height. This was found to be the case even in debilitated patients with advanced organic disease of the heart. Kny suggests that chloralamid is decomposed by the free alkali of the blood into chloral hydrate and formamid, but that this change takes place very slowly, and therefore but small quantities of chloral hydrate are liberated at a time. Moreover, it is conjectured that the depressant effect of the chloral is counteracted by the formamid, a member of the amido group, which has the property of stimulating the centres of the medulla oblongata. Drs. Hagen and Huefler in a careful study of a number of cases treated by means of chloralamid at the clinic of Prof. Struempell, of Erlangen, state that no adverse influences were noted in the heart's action, or respiration, temperature, digestion, or secretion of urine. Langaard, however, is of the opinion, on the strength of numerous experiments upon animals, that chloralamid does cause a marked depression of the circulation, and advises caution in its use in organic

* *Dublin Journal of Medical Science*, February, 1890.
† *Lancet*, October 26, 1889.
‡ *Deutsche Medicinische Wochenschrift*, No. 31, 1889.

diseases of the heart. * M. M. MAIRET and BOSE, also, in a communication to the Biological Society of Paris, assert that the drug exerts an influence upon the heart and reduces blood pressure. †

The chief physiological action is that of a hypnotic. In some instances this effect is produced within half an hour, in others it does not make its appearance until the lapse of two or three hours. In most cases, however, it is manifested within an hour. The slumber is sound, natural and refreshing, and continues from five to ten hours. As a rule no ill consequences are experienced upon awakening. Occasionally sleepiness persists upon the following day, and at times the effect of one dose is to break up the habit of sleeplessness for several successive nights. Languor, headache, vertigo, nausea, vomiting, thirst, incoherence, and cardiac depression have infrequently been noticed after large doses, but in no case have the manifestations been of an alarming character. No cumulative effects have been observed.

Therapy.—The chief therapeutic employment of chloralamid is in insomnia, except when insomnia is due to extreme mental excitement or severe pain. When sleeplessness is caused by or associated with nervousness, neurasthenia, hysteria, chronic alcoholism, and a great variety of organic affections, this remedy is usually productive of the happiest effects. The tastelessness of chloralamid, its comparative freedom from after-effects, its absolute safety in the number of cases in which it has been used, the absence of cumulative action or deleterious influence upon the secretions are advantages which cannot fail to commend this remedy alike to the therapeutist and the patient. So far as has yet been observed the existence of organic disease of the heart, lungs, liver, kidneys, brain or spinal cord constitutes no positive contra-indication to its administration. The conscientious practitioner is bound to watch with care the effect of any active drug which he may prescribe, and this truth applies to chloralamid just as it does to opium, chloral or nux vomica. Our experience with chloralamid is less than with chloral hydrate, yet it does appear that the former substance may be used with less dread and less danger than the latter when organic heart disease is attended by obstinate insomnia. Drs. HAGEN and HUEFLER remark that in cardiac asthma it seems

---

* *Medical Bulletin*, February, 1890, p. 57.

† *La Tribune Medicale*, June 12, 1890; *Medical Bulletin*, August, 1890, p. 285.

to have something akin to a specific power, and cite a case dependent upon arterial sclerosis, which had proved unamenable to morphine, in which 45 grains produced a deep sleep of 36 hours duration, and the paroxysms had not, at the time of publication, reappeared. In another case, one of constipation and senile disturbances dependent upon arterial sclerosis, the same writers observed a like beneficial effect. Dr. W. HALE WHITE has reported in the British *Medical Journal* twenty cases of various affections, among which were several of valvular disease, in which chloralamid was advantageously administered. KNY and REICHMANN met with the same experience. In the case of a boy suffering from pericarditis with mitral disease this drug was successfully used by W. HALE WHITE. The same writer mentions a case of thoracic aneurism in which chloralamid was more beneficial than hypodermic injections of morphine. Indeed, while it is in general true that chloralamid is of no avail when severe pain is present, yet exceptions to this statement are tolerably frequent. Pain was a prominent symptom in several of Dr. W. HALE WHITE's cases in which chloralamid was more efficacious than morphine in causing sleep. The affections were sarcoma of the rib, carcinoma of the stomach, carcinoma of the liver, rheumatic fever and floating kidney with mitral regurgitation, the floating kidney causing much pain. REICHMANN saw chloralamid of service in a case of sleeplessness due to gall stone, though the pains were not very violent. The same writer mentions a case of violent neuralgia in which chloralamid proved successful after morphine had failed. In herpes zoster and alcoholic neuritis pain has yielded to the soporific influence of this remedy, and Dr. CHARLES E. DENHARD, of New York, reports excellent results from thirty grain doses of chloralamid in cases of painful menstruation in young women.

In disease of the bronchial tubes, lungs and pleurae chloralamid is no less beneficial than in affections of the heart. In bronchial asthma, emphysema, pleurisy, and phthisis pulmonum suffering has been forgotten in sleep, and strength therefore conserved by means of chloralamid. This substance has been successful in overcoming wakefulness attendant upon cirrhosis of the liver, ulcer of the stomach, nephritis and pelvic disorders. In typhoid fever, erysipelas and diabetes the same symptom has been relieved by the same remedy. NAECKE commends the use of

chloralamid as a hypnotic in epilepsy and chronic mental disease
in women.   It may be safely used in any stage of paralysis.
Chloralamid allays restlessness and promotes sleep in chronic
mania and melancholia; in acute mania it either proves inefficacious or needs to be used in increased doses.   In cases of mental
alienation attended by extreme excitement the drug proved of but
slight avail.

Dr. MALSHIN, of Moscow, has published his experience with this
remedy in seventeen cases of various mental and nervous affections, in which it was administered 130 times in doses of thirty to
forty grains.   The best results were obtained in acute and chronic
paranoia, periodic psychosis, neuritis multiplex, and subacute articular rheumatism.   W. HALE WHITE records a case of brachial
monophlegia, probably due to embolism and cerebral softening,
and accompanied by noisy delirium, in which thirty grains of
chloralamid was always productive of several hours quiet sleep.
Dr. I. N. LOVE, of St. Louis, has derived excellent results from
chloralamid in the cerebral disturbances of children when other
agents had failed.   From two to four grains has produced good
sleep in an infant from six months to a year old, after chloral
hydrate and bromide of sodium had been tried in vain.   Dr. ALT.
of the Neurological Clinic at Halle, reports a very favorable result
from the use of chloralamid in two cases of chorea.   A boy, eleven
years of age, was almost completely cured in five days by the use
of fifteen grains three times a day.   The second case was that of a
girl who had been treated with arsenic for fourteen weeks without
result.   Recovery took place in eight days when placed on chloralamid.   Dr. C. R. HEXAMER, of Stamford, Conn., relates that in two
cases of alcoholic tremor he used chloralamid in doses of thirty to
forty-five grains with decidedly beneficial effect.   Several cases of
locomotor ataxia have been reported in which sleep was produced
by the same drug after the failure of morphine.   Comfortable sleep
followed its use in a case of spastic paraplegia under the care of
W. HALE WHITE.

In conclusion it may be mentioned as a valuable testimonial to
the worth of chloralamid that is has been made officinal in the last
edition of the German Pharmacopœia.

Philadelphia, Pa.

PHYSIOLOGICAL STUDY OF CHLORALAMID.

By H. C. Wood, M.D., LL. D.,

Member of the National Academy of Science ; Professor of Materia Medica and Therapeutics and of Diseases of the Nervous System in the University of Pennsylvania; Editor of the U. S. Dispensatory, etc.

and David Cerna, M. D., Ph. D.,

Assistant in Physiology in the University of Pennsylvania.

(Extract from Report of an Exhaustive Series of Trials.)

CONCLUSIONS.

Our researches have been made solely upon dogs, and therefore the following conclusions apply directly to those animals.

First. Chloralamid has a slight local influence, and in large doses tends to produce mucous diarrhoea.

Second. It acts more powerfully upon the cerebral cortex than upon any other portion of the nervous system of voluntary life, thereby causing sleep and muscular relaxation ; but it is also a feeble spinal depressant.

Third. It has a powerful influence upon the respiration, in moderate dose, by a centric action stimulating the respiratory rate, and probably also increasing the actual amount of air breathed; but in toxic dose causing death by paralysis.

Fourth. Its influence upon the circulation is a very feeble one; the changes produced by small doses being probably secondary to other effects of the drug; toxic doses, however, depress the arterial pressure by a direct action either upon the heart or upon the muscle coats in the arterioles.

THERAPEUTICALLY CONSIDERED.

The results of our experiments indicate that chloralamid is very worthy of trial as a hypnotic. Its action upon the heart is so slight that it bids fair to be valuable as a hypnotic in cases of feeble heart; whilst its stimulating influence upon the respiration would seem to fit it for employment in cases of nervous exhaustion. The exact clinical value of a hypnotic can, however, only be determined by clinical study. Dr. H. C. Wood has used the remedy to a moderate extent in various forms of insomnia, and so far it has seemed to him to be slower and less certain in its action than is chloral. Rarely have unpleasant after-effects been noted, but he has seen in some cases distinct headache. The statement of Hagen and Hüfler that the drug is especially valuable in cardiac asthma seems to be consonant with our experimental conclusions.

February 20, 1891.

Laboratory of Experimental Therapeutics,
University of Pennsylvania.

CHLORALAMID AS A HYPNOTIC.

By W. Hale White, M. D., F. R. C. P.,

Senior Assistant-Physician to, and Lecturer on Materia Medica and Theurapeutics
at Guy's Hospital.

From *British Medical Journal.*

In his exhaustive account[1] of many of the new hypnotics, Professor Leech says of chloralamid that the observations upon it are so far few in number. I have recently given it to twenty patients suffering from various illnesses, in all of whom insomnia was a troublesome symptom. Brief notes are appended. It will be seen that the drug produced comfortable sleep in all the patients except two; one of these was suffering from delirium connected with cerebral hemorrhage, and the other was admitted with rheumatic fever complicated by delirium tremens and salicylic poisoning. Both these patients died shortly after admission. It is noteworthy that some of the other patients were suffering from extremely painful diseases, and yet chloralamid produced sleep; thus a woman who had a thoracic aneurism preferred it to morphine, and another patient who had carcinoma of the stomach also slept better with chloralamid than with morphine. The patient with carcinoma of the liver suffered intense pain, yet she dozed comfortably after chloralamid. The man suffering from cerebral softening and who was quieted by the drug is also a striking case. Probably the house-physicians, sisters, and nurses are the best judges of hypnotics, as they see the patients frequently during the night. They all tell me that those who take chloralamid sleep well and comfortably after it, and the sisters of the three wards in which I have used it tell me that the *patients sleep better after chloralamid than after any of the hypnotics which have been introduced during the last few years.* My own experience, and what the patients themselves tell me, certainly agrees with this. In none of the twenty patients to whom I have given it—and many of them have taken several doses—have any effects followed that can be looked upon as contra-indications to its use. Never have I observed any depressing results, nor has headache followed its use. The time which elapses between its administration and the commencement of sleep varies between a quarter of an hour and two or three hours. If it is given in the even-

---

[1] *Journal*, November 2, 1889, p. 969.

ing, when once asleep the patient usually sleeps quietly till morning. Some writers have stated that occasionally after a dose in the evening the patient does not go to sleep till the next morning, and that he remains asleep all the day. This was so with one of my patients; but it must be remembered that, as the drug is feebly soluble in water—20 grains take five hours to dissolve in 2 ounces of water—it is often given as a powder with some milk. It was administered in this way to my patient who slept the next day, and I should think that some of these cases of delayed action were due to delayed absorption. Now I always prescribe it with spirit; 20 grains will dissolve in 1 drachm of rectified spirit in fifteen minutes, and water may be added to this solution without re-precipitating the drug. A good way of giving it is to tell the patient to dissolve it in a little brandy, add water to his liking, and drink it shortly before going to bed. If given in milk, not only is it insoluble, but it is difficult to swallow, for it sticks to the sides and bottom of the glass. The taste is slightly bitter, but by no means disagreeable. It should never be prescribed with alkalies, for they decompose it, nor should hot water be mixed with it, for it decomposes at 148° F. For an adult, 20 to 60 grains—the·exact amount depending upon the cause of the insomnia—is the dose; usually 30 grains will suffice. It has the advantage over sulfonal that it is only half the price, and it has the great advantage over paraldehyde that it has no nasty smell or taste, nor is it difficult to dissolve.

The few cases which have been published quite bear out the cases recorded here. It would seem that in chloralamid we have a safe hypnotic, which hardly ever has any depressing effects, which does not produce indigestion, and very rarely gives rise to any unpleasant results. We do not, of course, yet know what harm may result from its prolonged use. References to those authors who have studied the chemistry and physiological action of the drug will be found recorded by LEECH, PATERSON,[1] and in a leading article in the *Therapeutic Gazette* for September, 1889. RABOW[2] considers 45 grains of chloralamid to be equivalent to 30 grains of chloral. Chloralamid has been used successfully as an enema by PEIPER.[3]

---

[1] *Lancet*, October 26th, 1889.
[2] *Centralblatt für Nervenheilkunde*, August 1st, 1889.
[3] *Deutsch. Med. Woch.*, August 8th, 1889.

Case I.—Typhoid. A girl aged 4½. Very irritable and fretful, often keeps the other patients awake by her crying; 5 or 10 gr. of chloralamid always sent her to sleep a quarter of an hour after taking it. She slept quietly for many hours. She took it frequently for a fortnight.

Case II.—Sarcome of last rib, growing extensively into the tissues and organs around. A middle-aged man. He suffered intense pain, but 30 or 40 gr. of chloralamid always gave him sleep, often for the whole night. It relieved him as much as, or even more than morphine.

Case III.—Cerebral hæmorrhage with noisy delirium. An adult man. 30 gr. of chloralamid did not relieve the delirium.

Case IV.—Thoracic aneurysm; a woman. She suffered great pain. Before the introduction of chloralamid she was treated with injections of morphine. For the last month of her life she had many doses of 30 gr. or 40 gr. of chloralamid. She always slept well after it, and she said she preferred it to morphine.

Case V.—Subacute nephritis. A woman aged 27. Slept well and comfortably after a dose of 30 gr.

Case VI.—Mitral regurgitation, pericarditis. A boy aged 12. Slept all night after a dose of 5 gr.

Case VII.—Mitral regurgitation and albuminuria. A man aged 40. 30 gr. made him sleep well and comfortably.

Case VIII.—Extreme escites, probably due to cirrhoses. An elderly man much troubled with insomnia. 50 gr. made him sleep well and comfortably.

Case IX.—Carcinoma of the liver. A woman aged 38. She suffered extreme pain, but 30 gr. of chloralamid caused her to sleep well and doze in comfort.

Case X.—Erysipelas. A middle-aged woman. 30 gr. always made her sleep comfortably.

Case XI.—Rheumatic fever. A boy aged 10. 15 gr. every four hours gave him quiet sleep, although he suffered much pain.

Case XII.—Rheumatic fever, delirium tremens, salicylate poisoning. A man aged 40; died a few hours after admission. 60 gr. of chloralamid had no effect upon him.

Case XIII.—Brachial monoplegia, probably due to embolism and cerebral suffering. An old man, who was very noisy and delirious. 30 gr. always quieted him and produced sleep lasting some hours.

Case XIV. Mitral disease. A middle-aged woman. 30 gr. always produced sleep.

Case XV.—Carcinoma of the pylorus. A woman aged 56. 30 gr. always produced sleep better than morphine.

Case XVI.—Chronic eczema. A man aged 40. 30 gr. caused comfortable sleep.

Case XVII.—Mitral regurgitation and floating kidney. A woman aged 50.   30 gr. produced sleep, although the floating kidney caused much pain.

Case XVIII.—Spastic paraplegia. A woman aged 56.   20 gr. caused comfortable sleep.

Case XIX.—Phthisis, aortic disease, saturnine paralysis. A man aged 65.   20 gr. always produced sleep, but it took twelve hours to act, so that if the medicine were given in the evening the patient did not sleep during the night, but he slept all the next day.

Case XX.—Mitral regurgitation. An adult man. A severe case. 30 gr. produced comfortable sleep.

CHLORALAMID.

Editorial in *Medical Summary*, Philadelphia, Pa.

Chloralamid, a hypnotic, is one of the most recent products of the laboratory, and judging from the reports already published, we must infer that it promises to be one of the best of all the synthetic products which have been offered for this special purpose. Paraldehyde while useful, cannot be given to susceptible patients owing to its odor and nauseating taste; amylene hydrate is comparatively limited it its range of usefulness; and sulfonal is not always reliable; probably the most serious objection to chloralamid, as compared with chloral, is the size of the dose.   The matter of dosage, however, is not well settled, but it appears to be most efficient when given for the conditions in which chloral is used, if about one-half more is administered than the usual dose of chloral. The amount rarely exceeds thirty grains, and unlike chloral, it produces none of the bad effects on the following day, which are so characteristic of that drug.   Investigations thus far show that it does not have the effect of embarassing the circulation by depressing the action of the heart.   Few cases have been reported in which it was wholly useless, or in which untoward effects were produced, although it has been demonstrated that it cannot be depended upon when there is much pain.   In other words, it is a hypnotic, pure and simple, and does not partake of the properties of an anodyne.

The administration of this drug is adapted to all cases of insomnia, but more especially is it valuable in those cases due to organic disease, in which other hypnotics are often contra-indicated, and that class of cases characterized by unusual activity.   Disorders of the circulatory apparatus, respiratory neuroses, diseases of the nervous system, as well as the sleeplessness which occurs in the course of other diseases, as rheumatism, typhoid fever and organic and functional disorders of the alimentary tract, as ulcer, cancer and chronic dyspepsia.

Chloralamid occurs in the form of colorless crystals, soluble in nineteen parts of water and in one and one-half parts of alcohol, and although the taste is slightly bitter it may easily be disguised by the addition of a syrup or simple elixir. Being decomposed by alkalies, and not readily soluble in water, it is best given in the form of a solution along with a little wine, whiskey or brandy, to which is added a small amount of syrup. The following formula will prove serviceable :

R   Chloralamid ....З iv.
      Spts. vini gallici,
      Curacoæ, ãã partes equales ad.........................fl. З iv.
M. Sig.   A tablespoonful to be taken in water and repeated in four hours if required.

The advantage in using chloralamid is, that the influence of the drug will be sufficient to produce refreshing sleep for a period ranging from four to six or more hours, and that it does not show any special tendency to destroy digestion.

----->+<-----

CHLORALAMID AS A HYPNOTIC.

By Dr. George P. Cope.

Extract from the *Dublin Journal of Med. Science*, February, 1890.

I think these cases demonstrate that chloralamid is undoubtedly a sleep producing agent, that the sleep created varies from five to eight hours, and appears to be sound and refreshing. A dose of 25 to 35 grains was sufficient to cause sleep in patients suffering from melancholia and chronic mania, but in cases of acute mania small doses had no effect, and sleep was not produced by less than from 40 to 50 grains. No recognized evil effects followed the continued use of this drug for eight days; and only one out of twenty-five persons under treatment with chloralamid was noticed to be suffering from gastric disturbances—viz., giddiness and sickness, with dry, brown tongue, which followed six hours after a draught, when no sleep ensued.

In comparison with other hypnotics, chloralamid, as it consists of a combination of chloral, somewhat resembles it in its action. Both induce sleep, lasting from five to eight hours, but they appear to possess little analgesic influence unless when they cause sleep. Unlike opium they will not relieve pain. The time that elapses before sleep is produced varies from thirty minutes to an hour, and the sleep appears to be natural and refreshing. Its action on the circulation is stated to be quite the opposite of that of chloralhydrate, which acts directly upon the blood pressure, slowing the pulse and respiration, and producing poisonous effects by direct action on the cardiac ganglia and respiratory centre, causing paralysis of the heart and cessation of respiration. Chloralamid appears, as far as I have been able to ascertain, to be free from such danger. In five cases—one of pneunomia, one of phthisis, one of cardiac disease, and two of insomnia—I obtained sphygmographic tracings before and after its administration, and the blood pressure was not lowered in any of them, while the respiration and temperature remained the same. Dr. DANIEL LEECH *(British Medical Journal*, November 2, 1889), writing about chloralamid, states that "it seems probable that the formamide element, containing as it does a substitute NH group, will stimulate the circulatory and respiratory centres in the medulla, thus tending to counteract the depressing influence of chloral on them." REICHMANN noticed that with doses ranging from 30 to 60 grains the blood pressure was not lowered.

Comparing chloralamid with sulfonal, which has been extensively used in the Richmond District Lunatic Asylum, with very satisfactory results, for the last year and a half, I need not dwell upon the advantages of the latter as a hypnotic agent, because I have practically nothing to add to the observations made by Dr. CONOLLY NORMAN (see *Dublin Journal of Medical Science*, January, 1889), and fully confirmed by further experience. Speaking of sulfonal, Dr. NORMAN states that "its disadvantages are (1) that it is bulky and practically insoluble, therefore, difficult to administer, and that, perhaps, owing to its insolubility, (2) it is slow in action," and its price is high. Chloralamid, on the contrary, is not bulky, is tolerably soluble, quick in action (thirty minutes to one hour), and is now cheaper than sulfonal has ever yet become.

On the whole it seems that this new hypnotic is well worthy of a trial, having proved so far safe and reliable.— *M. and S. Journal.*

CHLORALAMID, A NEW HYPNOTIC.

From the *Medical Age.*

While at a first glance, it may seem quite superfluous to add another to the already long list of hypnotics, closer observation will show that this is not the case. Whilst, on the one hand, many lack promptness in action, on the other hand, many of those whose hypnotic action is rapid, are accompanied by such grave symptoms that their use can only be resorted to with extreme caution. The actual number of reliable, efficient, and, at the same time, safe hypnotics, is very small. The introduction of a new one, which promises to combine the above named desirable properties, should be joyfully welcomed rather than regarded as a superfluous addition.

Chloralamid, as introduced by v. Mering, is a product of anhydride of chloral (CCl_3CHO) and formamid ($CHONH_2$) and therefore has the formula

$$CCl_3CH<^{OH}_{NHCHO}.$$

It is a colorless crystalline substance, soluble in nineteen parts of water and in one and a half parts of alcohol (96 per cent.). Its taste is mild and slightly bitter, but not biting. The watery solution keeps well.

Dr. Ed. Reichmann reports quite a large number of cases in which he has used the drug; the dose given being almost invariably thirty grains. The hypnotic action was in all cases most prompt; sleep ensuing an hour after the dose had been taken. No unpleasant accompanying or after-effects were noted. The patients awoke the next morning refreshed and feeling as usual. Sphygmographic tracings were taken during the influence of the drug, but revealed nothing but normal heart action. Reichmann concludes that chloralamid is a safe and rapidly acting hypnotic, when given in doses of thirty to forty-five grains. Sleep ensues in half to three-quarters of an hour, seldom later. Its rapidity of action is, therefore, equal to that of sulfonal.

The absence of all unpleasant accompanying or after-symptoms. as well as the absence of any circulatory disturbances, will probably bring the drug into extensive use and make for it a place among the principal hypnotics

CHLORALAMID.

By JOHN AULDE, M. D.,

Demonstrator of Clinical Medicine, and lately Demonstrator of Physical Diagnosis, in the Medico Chirurgical College of Philadelphia.

From NOTES ON NEW REMEDIES.

In addition to the bromides, chloral, and the narcotic vegetable substances, we have a number of synthetic products that have lately been introduced as hypnotics, amongst which may be mentioned amylene hydrate, paraldehyde, urethan, uralium, sulfonal, hypnone, somnal, and the latest of all, chloralamid. To this comparatively recent product of the laboratory, I wish to call attention. Although a new substance, it has been used quite extensively, and with care, by a limited number of practitioners, principally those residing abroad. So recently has it been brought to the attention of physicians in this country, that but few reports have been published by American practitioners. The object of the present paper is to point out some of the indications and contra-indications for its employment, and at the same time to make some suggestions regarding its administration.

The indications for the exhibition of chloralamid naturally hinge upon its physiological action in disease as well as in health. When moderately large doses are given in health (45 to 60 grains), there is a decided effect upon the cerebrum. Headache, nausea, and giddiness, such as that seen after the ingestion of cannabis and belladonna, symptoms going to show that the effect must be due to the presence of the substance in the blood, by which the nervous system is affected. The drug cannot be recovered by washing out the stomach, a fact going to show that it is absorbed. Ordinarily the large doses do not affect the heart and circulation, although it has been noticed that the frequency of the pulse is slightly increased. These symptoms, it is said, are not of long duration, and are less marked than those following the exhibition of chloral. *The dose*, as compared with that of chloral, should be about one-half more, but it is rarely advisable to exceed thirty grains.

In diseased conditions of the system, chloralamid appears to be borne with a remarkable degree of tolerance, although some unfavorable results have been reported. It should also be borne in mind that it is useful only as a hypnotic to induce sleep, and cannot be depended upon to relieve pain. It has the advantage of being ready prepared, and is not objectionable to the palate, while the effect of the drug is manifested within a short time after taking, ranging from one-half to two hours, and fortunately, it continues for from six to eight hours. The after-effects, as a rule, are not objectionable.

Chloralamid has now been used with great benefit in a large number of diseases, organic and functional, where a hypnotic pure and simple was required, and if there be any special indications for its use over the hypnotics, two conditions might be named, that of insomnia attendant upon organic disease, and that connected with, or dependent upon, unusual excitement. Some of these diseased conditions may be noted as follows : Disorders of the circulatory system, as endocarditis, aneurism, cerebral hemorrhage, mitral insufficieny, and myocarditis. Respiratory neuroses, as phthisis, pneumonia and pleurolpneumonia, emphysema, bronchitis and bronchial asthma, and pleuritic exudation. Diseases of the nervous system, including such as tabes dorsalis, herpes zoster, intercostal neuralgia, neuralgia and cephalalgia, dementia paralytica, hysteria and sclerosis. Some general diseases which are not classified, as follows : Hepatic cirrhosis with ascites and cancer, alcoholism, contracted kidney, gastric ulcer, and cancer of the stomach, gonorrhœa, chronic constipation, erysipelas, rheumatism. eczema and other forms of skin disease, typhoid fever, and chlorosis.

Method of administration.— To obtain the best results from the use of chloralamid, certain precautions are necessary. Being insoluble in ordinary menstrua, and decomposed by alkalies and by heat (148 deg.), it should preferably be given in the form of a solution and within two hours after eating; by this means we insure its first coming in contact with the acid secretions of the stomach. When there are no moral objections, the drug can be combined with some form of spirit, as brandy or whiskey, as shown in the following formula :

```
R   Chloralamid ................................. ℥ iv
    Spts. frumenti ........................... fl. ℥ iii
    Elix. aurantii ....................q. s. ad fl. ℥ iv
```
M. Sig.   Take one tablespoonful in water every four to six hours, as directed.

It will be observed that each dose is intended to carry thirty

grains of the drug, but as some persons object to the taste of all
sorts of mixtures used for medicinal purposes, it may be necessary
occasionally to enclose the powder in a wafer or soft gelatine cap-
sule. Inasmuch as complaints have been made that when given
in the form of a powder, the effect of the drug is sometimes delayed
twelve or more hours, care must be exercised to determine the
condition of the stomach. For the reasons stated, therefore, the
powder should be administered a short time after taking food.

No accidents have been announced thus far, and but few
unfavorable reports, even with the very numerous and varied
classes of diseases treated, and everything points to its favorable
reception at the hands of the profession. It is to be hoped that
further investigations will prove equally satisfactory, and that no
attempts will be made to claim more for it than its virtues entitle
it to as a result of clinical observation.

1910 Arch St., Philadelphia, Pa.

------>+<------

CHLORALAMID A VALUABLE ADDITION TO THERAPEUTICS.

The following extracts are from an exhaustive paper just published by Dr. D. R. PATERSON (*Lancet*, October 26, 1889), and confirm in many respects the accounts published by Continental authorities:

"With the view of testing the efficacy of the new remedy, I have
given it in fourteen cases of insomnia, including simple sleeplessness and that resulting from phthisis, heart disease, enteric fever,
etc. . . I may say here that several observations were made on the
temperature, pulse, respiration, and urine, with a negative result.
Taking first the results in simple insomnia, we have four cases in
which the drug was given, two of them being above sixty years of
age. In one instance—an old woman of sixty-four, who had not
slept for some time, and used to spend the night by sitting up in
bed—30 gr. produced on consecutive nights, after an interval of
from thirty to forty minutes, a tranquil sleep of eight and nine hours
respectively. On both occasions there was some giddiness on
awakening, while on the second morning, in addition, she felt sick,
and remained drowsy during the forenoon. The dose being then
reduced to 15 gr., sleep did not result on an average earlier than

from half-an-hour to an hour and a half. It lasted, however, nearly eight hours and was free from any of the former unpleasant after-effects—in fact, after taking half-a-dozen doses, she stated her appetite was much better than it had been for some time. A man, sixty years of age, convalescent from an attack of jaundice, and complaining much of resting badly at night, received 30 gr. on several occasions. A sleep of eight hours, on an average, ensued in from forty to seventy-five minutes after administration. The sleep was unbroken, and very sound, and he declared it removed the dull headache from which he had been suffering. Here the drug was used on alternative evenings, and clearly showed its beneficial effects. In a woman, aged fifty, 30 gr. doses were followed by from seven to eight hours' sleep, and disappearance of paroxysmal cough, which was very troublesome. After the first dose there was next morning a feeling of sickness, but this, however, was not observed on any subsequent occasion. The fourth case was a man who had been carefully watched, and was absolutely sleepless for some days after his admission to hospital. Doses of 15 gr. to 30 gr. induced from two to four hours' rest on several occasions, and were sufficient to break, as it were, the sleepless habit. Its influence on the insomnia associated with phthisis, I found, on the whole, satisfactory. A night's rest of from six to seven hours frequently resulted from doses varying from 15 gr. to 40 gr.

"According to HAGEN and HUEFLER, chloralamid has in some cases no action on the insomnia of phthisis, while in others it produces considerable general malaise. The results obtained in two cases of heart disease were encouraging, and would compare favorably with those of any other hypnotic. Doses of 30 gr. in a man suffering from aneurism of the aorta gave fair rest, easing the pain and relieving the cough.

"Insomnia and restlessness resulting from pain were little, if at all, influenced by chloralamid. In two cases—one suffering from disease of the ankle with starting of the foot at night, and the other from dysentery with cramp-like pain in the abdomen—doses of 45 gr. caused, indeed, sleep, but with an attack of pain readily broke. From these few observations it would appear that the new hypnotic is not altogether free from some of the disadvantages attending those already in daily use. Doses of 30 gr. and 45 gr. have been followed by giddiness, feeling of sickness, dryness of the mouth, and even slight delirium—symptoms which, although not alarming, are certainly disagreeable, but which seem to be inseparable from the action of almost all our sleep-producing agents. A comparison of the action of chloral with that of the amide shows that the latter is not so rapid, sleep coming on half an hour to an hour after its administration; whereas after chloral it often results in fifteen minutes. This slight disadvantage, however, is more than compensated for by the almost entire absence of action which chloralamid has on the circulation."

Dr. PATERSON has paid special attention to the dose of this substance, and says:—"Usually 30 gr. to 45 gr. suffice in the case of a man, while 20 gr. to 30 gr. will give satisfactory results in a woman. In experiments carried out by ALT, 60 gr. produced in two strong healthy women severe giddiness, symptoms of intoxication, with great excitement, and in one great nausea and retching. Chloralamid has no action on the digestive organs, and the appetite remains unimpaired. That this drug will be a valuable addition to our therapeutical armamentarium is undoubted."

ON CHLORALAMID—A NEW HYPNOTIC.

By Prof. S. RABOW, M. D., Lausanne-Cery.

Centralblatt für Nervenheilkunde, DR. ERLENMEYER, No. 15, 1889.

In harmony with the thankworthy dissertation which my colleague JASTROWITZ has just delivered before the "Society for Internal Medicine" on the treatment of sleeplessness, I would like to direct your attention to an entirely new hypnotic which is worthy of consideration in more than one respect and which will probably find extensive employment in the future. I owe the same to the kindness of Prof. VON MERING, at whose instigation it was manufactured and placed in the market at a comparatively very moderate price. The remedy in question is chloralamid,—a combination of chloral and formamid. Numerous experiments on animals and human beings have proved that the remedy is capable of producing

sleep in moderate doses (1 to 4 g.). The sleep does not appear
as quickly as after the administration of chloral, but much sooner
than it does after sulfonal. I have never noticed an unfavorable
influence on the digestive organs.

In regard to its action of the vascular system, I have arrived at
no positive conclusion— this must be reserved till further experiments and observations have been made. The occasionally very
unpleasant and annoying after-effects of sulfonal are not experienced with chloralamid. Its comparatively great solubility is also
an advantage worthy of recognition.

As for the dose and mode of administration, my doses varied
from 1 to 4 grammes. I administered the re nedy in powder form
in wafers, also in wine and beer. It was taken with particular
pleasure in spiced wine.

As I learned—to my surprise—on a visit one morning, that the
remedy had effect only in one out of six different patients, it was
discovered, upon further inquiry, that the patient who had slept
well, had taken a powder containing 3 grammes, while the rest
had taken the chloralamid dissolved in boiling water as administered by the head nurse. By this procedure, the remedy was decomposed,—consequently the failure.

Having tried the above mentioned remedy on my own person
during a period in which I continually complained of insufficient
sleep, and having been well pleased with the effect of even 1 g.,
I was prompted to try the same on a number of insane patients
under my charge. It was proved that chloralamid must be given
in somewhat larger doses than chloral, and that 3 g. of the former
correspond in effect to 2 g. of the latter. Sleep usually followed
within 25 to 30 minutes after administration, and continued for 6 to
8 hours.

As a sedative for maniacs and highly irritable patients doses of
3 to 4 g. were entirely ineffectual. In the case of a quiet, sleepless
man, 3 g. chloralamid gave negative results, while 2 g. chloral
produced good sleep. On the other hand, the new remedy proved
reliable in the large majority of cases of sleeplessness from indulgence in alcohol, as well as in the so-called nervous sleeplessness, in neurasthenia, hysteria, etc. Up to the present day, I have
made 52 separate observations, among which but few failures can
be counted. Untoward collateral symptoms, I have not been ac-

quainted with. If such appear they can only be determined by more numerous observations. At all events, we may already regard the remedy as a worthy addition to our treasure of hypnotics.

CHLORALAMID.—A HYPNOTIC.

By Dr. J. M. Thompson.

The following cases will illustrate my somewhat limited experience with the new hypnotic, chloralamid. In all the cases in which I tried it, with one exception, the results were very encouraging and satisfactory. I usually give about 30 grains, in powder, dry, followed by milk, on account of its bitter and disagreeable taste.

Case I.—Mrs. M., 22 years; neurotic, subject to sleeplessness. Sulfonal caused an after-effect of lassitude and neutral hebetude; 30 grain doses of chloralamid at bed-time produced sleep within a half hour, without after-effects.

Case II.—Mr. G., 35 years; an habitué of morphine, which he has now almost wholly discarded. Since giving up the habit has not had a sound sleep. Chloral, bromides, and sulfonal produced no effect; 30 grains of chloralamid gave comfortable sleep of four to five hours' duration, with no unpleasant after-effects.

Case III.—Mr. D.; attack of "la Grippe," followed by delirium tremens; 30 grain doses of chloralamid, repeated three times at half-hourly intervals, produced but little sleep.

Case IV.—Young man, 27 years; nervous and restless from overwork. 30 grains of chloralamid produced profound sleep within 20 minutes.

Case V.—Mrs. G., 38 years; angina pectoris. Following an attack, 30 grains of chloralamid produced "sweet sleep" in a short time.

Case VI.—Man, 47 years; varicose ulcer; said, "chloralamid (30 grains) is the only drug which gives me sleep without causing debility."

Case VII.—Mrs. F.; alcoholic neuritis. Had not slept to any extent for months; 40 grains of chloralamid produced about two hours' sleep.

I can safely recommend chloralamid in any case where a hypnotic is indicated, and feel sure that it is the best, safest and most reliable in use up to date.

29 Hollis St., Boston, Mass.

PHYSIOLOGICAL ACTION OF CHLORALAMID.

Review of article in *Therapeutische Monatshefte.*

Dr. Eugen Kny, Assistant Physician of the clinic for mental diseases of the University of Strassbourg, publishes the results of his experiments with chloralamid.   He made special investigations with regard to the physiological action of the drug, and found that it possesses a decided hypnotic effect.   It proved quite harmless to the different animals experimented on. Further experiments resulted in the fact that :

Chloralamid in contra-distinction to chloralhydrat hardly alters the blood-pressure.

According to Cervello the difference between the blood-pressure before and after administration of chloralhydrate by the mouth amounted to 50 to 80 m. m., according to Kny's experiments with intravenous injection of chloralhydrate it amounted to 50 m. m.

With chloralamid the difference between the blood-pressure before and after internal administration or intravenous injection consisted of not more than 17 m.m., an amount which is within the normal boundaries of the oscillation of the blood-pressure in a perfectly natural sleep.

It appears from these experiments, that chloralamid in contra-distinction to chloralhydrate affects the heart's action only to a very slight degree.

After such preparatory experiments on animals it was quite justifiable to try the drug with patients suffering from insomnia.

The number of cases which Kny treated with chloralamid amounted to 31; more than 100 single doses were administered. The quantity given at the time varied between 20 and 60 grains. As it was Kny's object to study and compare the therapeutic value of chloralamid and chloralhydrate, he selected all those cases for the administration of chloralamid which from former experience were knowne to be beneficially influenced by chloralhydrate. They were mostly cases of ordinary insomnia.   In one case of severe mania chloralamid proved to be just as inefficacious as chloralhydrate.   In one case of excitatory melancholy both were tried without avail.   In a number of mental diseases, however, which were not accompanied by great excitation chloralamid proved to be equal in every respect to chloralhydrate. Such was his experience in 6 cases of melancholy, 2 cases of insanity of old standing, 2 cases of idiocy and 1 case of general paralysis with slight excitation. Two patients with chronic alcoholism and one with locomotor ataxy, who previously was accustomed to take pretty large doses of morphia, were invariably sent into a deep sleep by chloralamid.

Kny also obtained excellent results in cases of insomnia caused by organic affections, such as pulmonary consumption (one case), pleurisy (one case), heart disease (three cases), neuralgic pains of medium intensity (four cases) Cases of insomnia in advanced age may be treated by chloralamid without exposing the patient to the slightest risk. The action of chloralamid (in analogy to chloralhydrate) in cases of severe excitation of peripheric nerves, very intense pains or extremely distressing cough was only partial, as the author had the opportunity to observe in cases of very severe cephalalgia and intercostal neuralgia. In such cases the addition of a small dose of morphia is advisable.

The standard dose for chloralamid is slightly higher than for chloralhydrate, 45 grains of chloralamid being equal in their therapeutic effect to 30 grains chloralhydrate. Whilst with the latter sleep is usually produced within 15 minutes after its administration the hypnotic action of chloralamid usually does not set in before 20 to 40 minutes have elapsed.

Sleep produced by chloralamid is deep and refreshing. Its average duration varies between 6 and 10 hours. The patients in the morning wake with a perfectly clear head and without any troubles from the part of the digestive organs. Complaints of dimness of the head and unpleasant taste in the mouth so common after chloralhydrate have never been heard of after the administration of chloralamid.

With regard to the decided advantages which chloralamid posesses over chloralhydrate the following may be stated :

The complete absence of any unpleasant symptoms from the part of the digestive organs may be explained by the fact, that chloralamid does not irritate any mucous membrane. Whilst a 10% solution of chloralhydrate brought into contact with the conjunctiva produces intense hyperaemia an equally strong solution of chloralamid will not effect the delicate mucous membrane in the least. A similar observation may be made by placing a small particle of pure chloralhydrate on the tongue. This will cause an intensely bitter taste and burning sensation, whilst chloralamid applied in a similar way will only produce a slightly bitter taste which disappears rapidly.

Chloralamid is therefore readily taken even by the most delicate patients. It may be given in wafer or in water, or still better in wine or any other alcoholic beverage. No patient, not even those with weak stomachs or deranged state of digestion, need fear any ill effects from chloralamid.

To give chloralamid in some warm alcoholic beverage forms the most appropriate way of administering it, because it is most readily soluble in such liquids. Claret sweetened with a small quantity of sugar may be chosen if preferred.

The most important advantage of chloralamid consists in the fact, that the drug never affects the circulation, not even during the most profound sleep. The heart continues to beat vigorously and the blood-pressure remains nearly at its normal height. Evidence of this fact could be furnished in great variety, suffice it to cite the following instances : a patient of very weak constitution suffering from mitral regurgitation took chloralamid in pretty large doses (45 to 60 grains). Another patient suffering from advanced aortic regurgitation took similar doses. Both patients slept without interruption for 6 to 8 hours, and the heart's action was not in the least affected. Another patient went invariably through a stage of great excitation whenever he took chloralhydrate. After chloralamid he slept soundly, without any intermediate excitatory symptoms. This has probably to be explained by chloralamid beeing completely devoid of any paralyzing effect on the cerebal bloodvessels. Patients who took chloralamid never showed any symptoms of congestion of the head, nor did they ever complain of any unpleasant sensation in the head.

The observation that chloralamid, quite contrary to chloralhydrate, hardly influences the circulatory organs may be explained by two reasons :

Chloralamid circulating with the blood is separated by the free alkali of the latter into chloralhydrate and formamid. The decomposition is effected very gradually and therefore only very small quantities of chloralhydrate act at one time.

Secondly, the other component of chloralamid, formamid, represents like all substances belonging to the amid group a powerful stimulant of the vasomotory centre in the medulla, and therefore greatly helps to keep the blood-pressure at its normal level.

The difference between the action of the two closely related bodies, chloralamid and chloralhydrate, may briefly be recapitulated thus : chloralhydrate is a stronger hypnotic than chloralamid, and can therefore not be dispensed in cases where a very powerful and rapidly acting sleep-producer is required. Chloralamid, however, possesses distinct advantages over chloralhydrate, namely : it tastes better and is therefore more readily taken; it does not influence the heart nor does it affect the digestive organs. Signs of congestion of the head and other unpleasant after-effects, frequently observed after chloralhydrate, never occur after chloralamid.

The author also made comparative experiments to illustrate the action of chloralamid and sulfonal. He came to the conclusion that in the majority of cases chloralamid acted much better than sulfonal. A number of intelligent patients who were perfectly competent judges repeatedly assured him that after frequent trials with both drugs they arrived at the conclusion that chloralamid is much preferable to sulfonal. Chloralamid excels sulfonal in solubility, it causes sleep which sets in very soon after its administration, and which is sure to pass off the next morning, whilst with sulfonal the patients often have to wait for several hours until they obtain the desired repose, which is, however, frequently unnecessarily prolonged during part of the following day.

Chloralamid may therefore confidently be recommended as a very powerful, reliable and harmless hypnotic.

Its use is indicated in the following cases of insomnia :

1.—Nervous excitation of a slight degree.

2.—Neurasthenia.

3.—Insomnia as a consequence of organic lesions, such as pulmonary consumption, heart disease, spinal affections, etc.

4.—All other cases of insomnia which are not the consequence of violent physical pain or severe exitation of the nervous system.

ON CHLORALAMID—A NEW HYPNOTIC.

By Dr. ED. REICHMANN,

Assistant Physician at the Medical Clinic of Prof. RIEGEL, Giessen.

Deutsche Medicinische Wochenschrift, No. 31, 1889.

Although it may seem superfluous at first sight,—considering the proportionately large number of hypnotics—to busy ourselves with new ones and to foster the introduction of the same, we must nevertheless come to the conclusion upon close critical study of the individual remedies, that such action, at all events, cannot prove useless.   On the one hand, not all of them have the prompt action which is expected from a hypnotic, on the other hand, those that have a good and positive effect, have by-effects besides which contra-indicate their employment in certain cases; in any individual case, the choice is consequently not so wide as it seemed at first.

Very willingly did I respond to the request of Prof. RIEGEL to experiment with a new hypnotic, chloralamid, prepared by E. SCHERING, of Berlin.   I began my experiments by administering to a medium-sized dog 3 grammes—the dose stated to produce sleep in adults—by way of the oesophagus.   I intentionally selected a comparatively large dose in order to determine whether the remedy had any ill-effects.   During the period immediately following, nothing particular was noticed in the animal, and only after about $1\frac{1}{2}$ hours it appeared tired and sleepy, without really falling asleep, however.   Untoward consequences were not observed.

Although this experiment gave almost a negative result, it gave no evidence against the efficiency of the remedy on the human being.   In my subsequent experiments on the human being, on the contrary, it was proved that chloralamid must be regarded as a most useful effectual hypnotic free from unpleasant after-effects.

In making my experiments, I observed in most cases the precaution recently fully presented by O. ROSENBACH—in leaving the patients in the dark as to the effect of the remedy, or where the patient had become acquainted with the same, in making controlling tests with inert substances.

I commenced with the administration of 1 grm. chloralamid. The results varied, the influence being always slight; in a robust patient with multiple sclerosis, I observed no effect; in others, in weakened individuals, particularly in a case of phthisis, little effect. The latter slept better during the night than usual, but still quite poorly. The following day I gave as a test a powder containing only saccharum album (in wafers) and talked about hypnotics, but the patient did not sleep better than usual. By day I could produce the feeling of fatigue and sleepiness with 1 grm. chloralamid, but no sleep. The dose was consequently increased to 2 grm. producing a distinct influence which brought out the sleep-producing properties of chloralamid prominently, although the success with this dose was not always a very prompt one. A few examples may verify this:

1. Caroline F., 27 years; bronchitis, cephalalgia.—At 8 o'clock in the evening, 2 grm. chloralamid administered.—Fell asleep before 9 o'clock, and did not awake till 6 in the morning. Formerly complained of poor sleep; condition the next morning the same as on previous days.

2. Elizabeth H.—24 years of age; chlorosis, mitral insufficiency. At 8 o'clock in the evening, 2 grm. chloralamid administered. Got tired soon after and felt dizzy upon getting up later (to close the window), fell asleep after ¾ of an hour, and slept the whole night without awaking. Felt well in the morning, no after-effects.

3. Wm. K.—42 years; endocarditis aortae et mitralis. Complained of sleeplessness, did not sleep well the preceding night, not even after a dose of morphine (only ⅛ grain, it is true). This evening (June 25th) at 8:30 o'clock, 2 grm. chloralamid were administered. Fell asleep about 10 o'clock, slept—with but one short interruption, at 11 o'clock—till 6 o'clock in the morning. No after-effects. patient enraptured with the remedy.

4. The same patient. 2 grm. chloralamid administered 8 o'clock in the evening. Sleep was not as good as on the 25th, but better than usual.

5. The same patient. At 9:30, 2 grm. chloralamid administered. Fell asleep at 10 o'clock, awoke at 3 o'clock, upon the entrance of the night-watch, but was sound asleep when the nurse entered at 2 o'clock. After 3 o'clock, he slept till morning. Condition in the morning the same as usual. The next day a controlling test was made on the same patient with 2 grm. sulfonal. (8:30 P. M.) He went to sleep 1½ hours later, slept uninterruptedly till 4 o'clock in the morning, was so tired and indisposed the next day, that he did not desire any hypnotic.

The same observation,—that, after chloralamid, the condition of the patient on the following morning was better than after sulfonal, effect having been the same otherwise—I made on two other patients; both fell asleep at nearly the same time after the administration of chloralamid as after sulfonal, the sleep lasted about the same length of time; after the former, they felt as well as usual—after the latter, some complained of giddiness and lassitude, others of slight transient nausea. If 2 grm. chloralamid were administered during the day, they did not always succeed in producing real sleep, but nevertheless provoked the feeling of fatigue and sleepiness; in somewhat run down, weakened individuals, sleep supervened also by day. For example:

I. Minna K.—33 years of age; ecstasia ventriculi. At 5:45 in the afternoon, 2 grm. chloralamid were administered. Patient got sleepy towards 6:30, but did not fall asleep till 9 o'clock, and then slept through till morning.

II. Elizabeth J.—19 years; chlorosis. In the afternoon at 1:45 o'clock, without informing the patient of the nature of the powder, 2 grm. chloralamid were administered, while she was up out of bed. At about 2:45 o'clock she complained of tiredness, dizziness, sleepiness and headache and wanted to go to bed. But she was persuaded not to do so, and consequently retired only shortly before the doctor's visit at 5 o'clock, in accordance with the rules of the house. She fell asleep, awoke at 6:00 when visited, fell asleep again, and slept, with but a few short interruptions, till morning.

III. Maria Z.—20 years; chlorosis. At 12:30 P. M., 2 grm. chloralamid administered. Fell asleep about 1 o'clock, awoke at 4 o'clock, continued tired and sleepy until 7 o'clock. The following night the patient did not sleep well, presumably on account of pain in the left ear. No collateral symptoms.

Equally satisfactory, in fact more so, were the results from doses of 3 grm. The latter succeeded in most cases in putting the patients, who had not the faintest idea that they had taken a hypnotic, to sleep by day also. I will not relate the clinical histories in detail, to avoid being tedious, but desire to emphasize the fact that the remedy succeeded in producing sound sleep in two drunkards who had suffered from obstinate insomnia. In the first of these cases, .01 grm. morphine had hardly any effect. In the second, I gave an inert powder the next day as a controlling test, whereupon the patient slept just as poorly as usual. It was, therefore, clearly proved that the mind plays no important part in producing the sleep brought on by chloralamid.

Worthy of mention furthermore is the fact that chloralamid also proved effectual in several cases in which pain was the cause of the sleeplessness, as in a woman with gallstone colic, in whom the pains were not very violent. The patient fell asleep at half past one o'clock,—about ¾ of an hour after taking 3 grm. chloralamid. To another patient who had persistent violent neuralgic pains, for which she had taken morphine repeatedly, but nevertheless slept poorly, I gave, instead of the customary dose of morphine, 4 grm. chloralamid at 11 o'clock in the forenoon. She slept soundly from half past eleven to half past two o'clock, after that she was in a rather semi-dormant condition. I occasionally observed slightly disagreeable symptoms, when the powder had been given during the day, and the onset of the sleep had been somewhat retarded, in which instances the patients complained of slight headache. On a few occasions, the patients still felt tired and sleepy upon awakening the next morning.

Although the question, whether chloralamid has a sufficient hypnotic influence to be employed therapeutically with success, must be answered positively in the affirmative, there still remains a vastly more important question to be answered, namely, whether there is any influence exerted on the circulation of the blood. The experiments made in this direction (in 11 cases) *proved that no such influence can be noticed from 2 to 4 grm. doses.* Let me give an example.

CURVE I.

CURVE II.

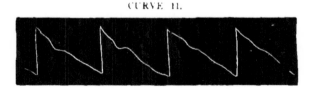

CURVE III.

CURVE IV.

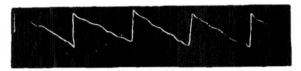

CURVE V.

As a comparison, I should like to add two sphygmograms—one taken *before*, the other, an hour *after* 3 gr. chloralhydrate had been given—which show the change to the blood pressure effect by the latter agent, as contrasted with the above.

CURVE VI.

CURVE VII.

While we notice no material change in curve I. to V. with chloralamid, we notice in the last two (VI. and VII.) with chloralhydrate a weakening in the elevation of expansion, a sinking of the elevation of contraction,—signs of diminished arterial tension and diminished blood pressure. Measured with a v. Basch sphygmomanometer, no considerable fluctuation in the pressure of the blood was noticed with chloralamid. Whether possibly patients become accustomed to chloralamid, cannot be determined as yet, considering the short time it has been in use.

Although we still can form no conclusive opinion from what has been said about chloralamid, we may venture to say that the same fulfills all the requirements of a hypnotic. 1.—Safe, prompt action followed doses of 2 to 3 grm., sleep supervening after ½ to ¾ of an hour, sometimes a little earlier, seldom later (just as soon as after sulfonal); 2.—The absence of annoying and under circumstances contra-indicated by-effects,—inasmuch as the patients felt well subjectively upon awaking, and objectively no change in the circulation of the blood was observed.

ON THE HYPNOTIC EFFECT OF CHLORALAMID.

By Dr. HAGEN and Dr. HUEFLER,

Assistants at the Clinic of Prof. STRUEMPELL, Erlangen.

Muench. Med. Wochensch., No. 30, 1889.

Most readers will view the introduction of a new hypnotic with considerable mistrust, as there is probably no such remedy which has eventually, after thorough examination and continued use, justified all the claims of superiority made in the beginning by its introducers.

In judging the value of a hypnotic it is necessary to be particularly cautious, as so many factors combine in the producing of sleep which cannot be controlled, some of which are even unknown, that it becomes difficult to determine the actual effect of the remedy employed.

A great variety of remedies are in use for producing sleep, and each of them is successful in some cases while totally ineffectual in others. One patient will sleep on the application of a cold bandage around his neck; another requires chloral hydrate; a third will slumber by suggestion. It is certainly a fact that suggestion must be considered as a factor in producing such sleep: as an instance, we have a patient in our clinic, suffering from chronic myelitis, who will sleep only after the administering of a hypnotic; the dose consists merely of 2 grammes saccharum album.

It is not to be inferred from this, however, that every hypnotic acts on this assumption.

There are two kinds of hypnotics: the one is a physiological aid in producing sleep (for instance, sulfonal); the other produces it artificially (to which class belongs morphine, and probably chloral). The division, however, cannot be accurately determined. Even the action of remedies of the second class is not always a positive one, and if successful the psychical condition as a factor must not be lost sight of. Consequently the action of hypnotics is often unreliable, and every remedy, though furnishing at times the most satisfactory result, will at other times fail entirely of the desired effect.

The demand for an hypnotic of reliability—a desideratum occurring so very frequently in practice—has by no means yet been filled. Not one of the new remedies, introduced of late—not excepting sulfonal—has realized the expectations hoped for at the time of introduction.

We consequently undertook our experiments with chloralamid, at the request of Professor STRUEMPELL, without much hope of its proving of value. Our experiences, however, proved so encouraging and apparently so conclusive, that we no longer hesitate, in view of our experiments, to pronounce it *one of the most reliable of hypnotics known to us.*

If we were to rank it with the two classes mentioned above, we would count it with those directly producing artificial sleep. That no physical condition or suggestion entered into the effect during our trials, is shown by the fact, as will be noted in the history of the cases to be furnished later on, that the Chloralamid was usually administered without the patient's knowledge. The positive effect is also testified to by the circumstance that the sleep lasted far into the morning, and that patients on awakening still gave signs of sleepiness, although the clearness of the mind was not weakened or dulled.

It should be stated here that the remedy, where its action was at all satisfactory, produced sleep one-half hour after administration.

Our experiments extended over a considerable period and the observations on individual cases are briefly noted in the following; the first two were cases of cardiac affections:

I. Johanna Z., 58 years of age; mitral insufficiency with severe chronic nephritis, general anasarca, and symptoms of dyspnoea. This patient, who slept very poorly without the aid of artificial means and was not benefitted to any extent even by morphine, received chloralamid ten times in all, sometimes in 3 and partly in 2 g. doses. No ill by-effects whatever were noticed; patient always slept soundly the whole night; it is worth mentioning that she also slept the greater part of the following morning. On only one occasion the patient suffered from headache in the morning.

II. Regina H., 69 years; myocarditis dependent upon arterial sclerosis. To relieve severe attacks of cardiac asthma which disturbed her sleep very much, and against which morphine had proved quite ineffectual, a single dose of 3 g. of chloralamid was administered with the result that she slept 36 hours without eating or awakening. She slept so soundly that she could be washed and have her toilet arranged without waking up. After a brief awakening she slept for 8 hours more. Particularly noteworthy is the fact that the attacks of cardiac asthma have not reappeared since. The patient remarked: "This sleep the dear Lord gave me."

The remedy was furthermore employed in a series of cases of diseases of the nervous system:

III. Catherine H., 62 years; tabes dorsalis in the highest degree with severe lancinating pains between the shoulder blades. Patient had only interrupted sleep after taking morphine, and complained bitterly of pains during the intervals. Chloralamid was administered in doses of 2 g. sixteen times in all. As a result she invariably slept the entire night without interruptions, sometimes until late in the morning. On one occasion, her supply of chloralamid being exhausted, she took morphine and in consequence slept very poorly. On one occasion only did she complain of headache the morning after taking chloralamid.

IV. Anna W., 42 years; tabes dorsalis with pains in the joints. Patient suffered for some time from sleeplessness, but slept the whole night and following forenoon after a dose of 3 g. chloralamid; besides a slight headache early in the morning no untoward symptoms supervened.

V. Franz X. R., 63 years; tabes dorsalis with lancinating pains in the limbs. Patient had long suffered from sleeplessness for which morphia afforded only moderate relief; 3 gr. chloralamid induced uninterrupted slumber, lasting far into the next day with only brief intervals. Chloralamid was administered fifteen times in all and uniformly successful, although the relief from pain did not extend to the time of wakefulness. 2 g. produced sleep during the night, but the influence did not extend into the next day. The patient remarked: "That is an excellent remedy." In one instance no chloralamid was given and the patient in consequence slept as poorly as formerly. No ill-effects.

VI. Kunigunda W., 67 years; herpes zoster with severe intercostal neuralgia and consequent unyielding sleeplessness. 3 g. chloralamid induced sound slumber all night and late into the morning, the patient wondering "what had become of the night." 2 g. doses afforded only a few hours sleep.

VII. Xavier H., 17 years; myelitis acuta transversa of eight weeks' standing. Patient slept poorly at night, probably in consequence of considerable disturbance of respiration due to paralysis of the intercostal muscles; morphine was not always effectual. No definite success was attained with 3 g. of chloralamid; after a second 3 g. dose the patient slept a trifle better, but still with frequent interruptions; a third trial of the same dose without result; a final experiment with 3 g. resulted in good sound sleep, without ill-effects.

VIII. Franz J., 46 years; dementia paralytica. Patient was often very restless during the night, and sleep was frequently interrupted. 3 g. chloralamid produced no sleep; patient arose during the night and complained of headache; applied cold poultices, but headache continued until morning. A second administration of chloralamid proved fruitless, but provoked no unpleasant collateral symptoms.

IX. Maria R., 40 years; hysteria with palpitations of the heart and sleeplessness. Patient took 2 g. nine times in all, and always slept well in consequence without experiencing any ill-effects whatever. When she left she insisted on taking several doses with her.

X. Sophie S., 83 years; haemorrhagia cerebri dextra; slept very poorly but refused to take a hypnotic. Without her knowledge, therefore, 2 g. chloralamid were administered in wine, producing sleep which lasted through the night and half the next morning, and for the rest of the day—as she said herself—she continued to feel tired and sleepy; no ill-effects.

XI. Margarette E., 35 years; affectio apicis sinistri with pleuritis sinistra. Patient had habitually taken morphine to induce sleep, being much disturbed by coughing fits at night, but its influence was insufficient. Chloralamid was administered eleven times, partly in 3 g. and partly in 2 g. doses, and patient invariably slept exceedingly well in consequence; as the effect of the hypnotic extended even to the next day and night she evinced active desire to continue the doses. Beyond feeling very hungry after awakening, no attending phenomena were noted.

XII. Peter G., 18 years; rapidly progressing phthisis. Slept poorly after taking morphine which had been prescribed to relieve a violent attack of coughing. On administering two 3 g. doses chloralamid patient slept soundly till morning and continued sleepy even then; the sleep was disturbed only once by coughing.

XIII. Michael T., 40 years; phthisis in the last stages and pleurisy on the side. Patient's sleep had been very poor for some time back; four doses of chloralamid were given in all; 3 g. and even 2 g. doses produced sound sleep lasting until morning. On one occasion the patient had slight delirium toward morning, but this must be regarded as due to debility, as the patient had previously had similar attacks when no chloralamid had been administered.

XIV. Hans L., 29 years; extensive phthisis complicated with haemorrhagic nephritis; patient slept poorly even after large doses of morphine. After a 3 g. dose of chloralamid he slept soundly all night, and far into the next day with only brief interruptions; on awakening finally he had abundant expectoration, due to the fact that the sleep had only once been broken by coughing. 2 g. doses induced sleep lasting through the night; after the third 2 g. dose he had a morning temperature of 35.40° C. (95.70° F.) complained of great weakness, and of lightness in the head; at the time we ascribed these symptoms to the hypnotic, but they were also present the following day when no chloralamid had been taken. After a fourth dose of 3 g. there ensued no reduction of temperature, but the patient felt weak and miserable in the morning.

XV. George M., 16 years; phthisis in the last stage; in spite of morphine sleep was very poor and much disturbed by coughing. 3 g. chloralamid were not positively successful, and patient complained of slight headache in the morning; 3 g. in wafers were vomited; 3 g. in wine were unsuccessful and produced slight headache.

The following cases pertain to various diseases:

XVI. Andreas W., 56 years; emphysema, left-sided pleurisy; patient never slept well after taking morphine. Chloralamid was administered seven times in all; 2 g. and 3 g. doses were equally successful. Patient always had headaches for half-an-hour in the morning after taking the chloralamid, but was so satisfied with its hypnotic effect that he declared himself "ready to stand three times the headache rather than dispense with the remedy." Patient was inclined to exaggerate in praising his new sleep-producer.

XVII. Friedrich P., 53 years; cirrhosis of the liver; a strong drinker; always very restless at night and sleep frequently interrupted. Chloralamid in 3 g. doses produced sound slumber which lasted until morning; no attending symptoms.

XVIII. Joseph N., 34 years; heavy drinker. Owing to diminished indulgence in alcohol while at our clinic the patient had poor and restless sleep. Two doses of 3 g. chloralamid each were successful and without ill-effects.

XIX. Johann B., 51 years; large ulcus ventriculi; patient had always slept poorly in spite of morphine. He took chloralamid eight times; 3 g. doses ensuring sleep which lasted the greater part of the following day even without interruption. The following two evenings he took 1 g. doses; the first night his sleep was much interrupted, and the second night he hardly slept at all. 2 g. doses again produced sound, refreshing sleep, and only once was there an interruption, due to violent vomitting.

XX. Veit S., 41 years; trichinosis. Patient had slept but four hours a night since the beginning of the disease, and even then with numerous interruptions. After a dose of 3 g. chloralamid he slept 8 hours uninterruptedly, but complained of lightness and slight pain in the head, with depression, lasting until evening; for this reason patient preferred not to take the hypnotic.

XXI. Johann W., 30 years; encysted pleuritic exudation; patient did not sleep particularly well with morphine. On taking 2 g. doses of chloralamid he slept quietly until morning, with almost no interruption; no collateral symptoms.

XXII. Heinrich M., 23 years; chronic gonorrhoea and cystitis; patient complained that his sleep was frequently broken during the night. On taking 3 g. chloralamid patient slept soundly and continued to feel tired and sleepy all the morning following; no collateral symptoms.

XXIII. Wolfgang H., 29 years; scorbutis; patient complained of greatly interrupted sleep. Chloralamid in 3 g. doses produced sound and restful sleep all night; no by-effects.

XXIV. Adam K., 82 years; chronic constipation and arterial sclerosis (senile disturbances). Patient, who subsequently received five doses of chloralamid, had previously slept very poorly at night; 3 g. gave him sound sleep lasting the whole night and far into the morning with but short breaks; 2 g. produced a sound night's rest, with no secondary symptoms. Patient praised the remedy in the highest terms and urged repetitions constantly; he "would not like to do without it."

XXV. Sybilla F., 39 years; contracted kidneys, with severe (uræmic) headaches; patient slept very poorly and constantly moaned from pain. The first 3 g. dose of chloralamid produced very good sleep lasting into the forenoon; the second dose gave the same favorable result, with no collateral symptoms.

In the foregoing detailed cases the experiments were made with reference to the action of chloralamid or actual sleeplessness. To determine the objective influence of the hypnotic it was now tried on three nearly cured patients (ulcus molle) who had slept well the preceding nights. They had no idea of the nature of the medicament, believing it a remedy for their sickness. The result of a dose of chloralamid was pronounced languor and drowsiness, compelling two of the patients to quit the usual housework at which they had been employed while convalescing; the effect of the hypnotic was manifested within one hour, and sleep lasted the entire day with only infrequent interruptions, due to the sky-larking of neighboring patients who ridiculed the laziness and drowsiness of their comrades.

Our experiments were confined to 25 sick and 3 convalescing patients, 28 cases in all, with 118 single doses. Decided hypnotic action followed in 26 cases, in 16 the result being strikingly effective, and in the balance comparing favorably with o her hypnotics. Negative results were evidenced in only two cases,—in the case of dementia paralytica, and in very grave phthisis. In the case of acute myelitus (VII.) its influence was doubtful.

A comparison between chloralamid and chloral, based on our observations so far, would indicate preference for the former on account of manifest superiority. In the first place, the taste of chloralamid is more agreeable than that of chloral; secondly and of great importance, the hypnotic action of chloralamid is decidedly greater than that of chloral; and finally, the side-effects are doubtlessly milder in the administration of chloralamid. So far as these side-effects are concerned, moreover, only slight pain and lightness in the head after awakening were noted, and these were present only eight times in the twenty-eight cases reported. In one case (XI.) a constant feeling of hunger resulted after awakening, and in another there was a collapse, but this could not justly be referred to the influence of chloralamid.

It should be remarked that we administered the hypnotic frequently and continuously to some of the patients (cases I., III., V. and XI.), and it was established by the fact that no diminution of the hypnotic effect was evinced that patients do not become accustomed to it nor does the remedy lose its power of action. This fact speaks forcibly against a mere psychological influence of the medicament. It has too often been shown that other hypnotics, while effective to the expected and desired degree with the first dose or doses, soon lose all action except in increased doses, and sometimes altogether.

We should also remark particularly that chloralamid has no specific influence on pain or other symptoms of disease. Only in cardiac asthma it seemed to have a somewhat specific therapeutic effect, especially in case II., where the pulse, which had been very poor, rose considerably during the action of the hypnotic, and remained good.

This leads us to the application of chloralamid in separate forms of disease. As far as possible with the opportunities at our clinic, we employed the hypnotic preferably on patients with severe organic affections, on whom hypnotics generally operate with less certainty than in cases of purely nervous physical sleeplessness; and it rendered uniformly good service in patients with organic nervous diseases, as in those with pulmonary complications, cardiac affections, or kidney derangements. It is specially desirable that further investigation be made in a large number of cases of purely nervous sleeplessness, as a clinic naturally affords little opportunity for treating such phases. The remedy was also decidedly effective in sleeplessness aggravated by intense pain.

As for dosage, 2 g. seemed sufficient in most cases, especially in women; in severe cases 3 g. should be the proper dose. The mode of administration was preferably by wafers, or dissolved in wine; no difference in effect was noted, however taken. As has been intimated no adverse influences were noted in the heart's action, or respiration, temperature, digestion, or secretion of urine.

In conclusion, we desire to give unqualified recommendation to chloralamid as a useful hypnotic. It is true that in a few cases within our experience it failed of action, perhaps in wider practice some untoward by-effects may even be attributed to it, and ill symptoms may develope from long continued use of it; but from the observations made and deduced from our experiments we conclude that chloralamid must be ranked with the most valuable hypnotics heretofore employed. For the general practitioner, who is often obliged to change medication during the progress of his patients' conditions, it will be a specially advantageous adjuvant: it is moreover moderate in cost, an advantage over similar late hypnotic introductions, besides exerting superior influence.

VERY EFFECTUAL, SAFE, AND PLEASANT TO TAKE.

S. A. K. Strahan, M.D., L.R.C.P., Barrister-at-law; Assistant Medical Officer to the County Asylum, Northampton (*Lancet*, February 15th, 1890) says, in summing up the results of his clinical trials in 23 cases :—

1.—Chloralamid is a very effectual hypnotic.

2.—It appears to have no depressing effect whatever on the heart.

3.—The dose is about 35 to 45 grains; but 55 grains may be given with safety.

4.—It should be administered an hour or an hour and a half before the time sleep is desired.

5.—Its action is in some cases deferred so long as three hours, even in cases where it gains prolonged sleep.

6.—No ataxic symptoms or headache follow its use.

7.—It does not affect the digestive system.

8.—It is a very useful and safe hypnotic, and may be given to paralytics whatever their stage.

9.—In my opinion it is equal, but in no way superior, to paraldehyde, save that it is much pleasanter to take, and does not impart to the breath any such disagreeable odor as does the latter drug.

CHLORALISM.

By J. B. MATTISON, M. D.

Medical Director Brooklyn Home for Habitués. Member Amer. Med. Assn.,
Amer. Assn. for the Cure of Inebriety, N. Y. Academy of Medicine,
N. Y. Medico-Legal Society, N. Y. Neurological Society,
Medical Society of the County of Kings.

Original Communication for NOTES ON NEW REMEDIES.

CHLORALISM has largely waned in the last half decade. The advent of other—though not better, in some respects, I am bound to say—hypnotics has lessened the growth of a toxic disease that, ten years ago, bade fair to assume large proportions and wreck some of the best in the land. Its victims came mainly from the educated rank of our people,—brain workers,—those who by super-zealous devotion to duty, or long and exhausting vigils over mental toil, had banished the "sweet restorer." Many chloral inebriates were found among the large and—at that time more than now—enlarging number of morphine habitués, who were impelled to its use by the inroads of the poppy along insomnic lines.

So, too, among rum-takers, the marvellous power of chloral in wooing the drowsy god, after a big debauch, led to its use—with or without medical counsel—that, at times, could only be called reckless, and that again and again brought the long lost sleep.

Besides the risk of confirmed addiction from the uncareful use of chloral, it has a pernicious power *per se* that is unique,—greater than morphine, though the latter is more snareful and more difficult to cure. Regarding this effect, along various lines—psychic and somatic—no more complete picture has ever been presented than that by the writer, eleven years ago, in a paper—"Chloral Inebriety"—read before the Medical Society of the County of Kings, April 15th, 1879, (at command of anyone who may desire and will write for a copy), which contains a striking case, akin to the one presented in this paper, noting a special effect of chloral, and mainly peculiar to that drug.

Quoting from that paper,—"I refer to peculiar pains in the limbs, simulating neuralgia or rheumatism; yet unlike the former as they are not limited to the course of the nerves, and differing from the latter in not being exactly *in* the joints, but rather *girdling* the limbs just above or below them, without pain on pressure, and unaggravated by movement. Their diagnostic import is that they may be mistaken for the diseases they resemble, and their origin being unsuspected, prove obstinate to treatment."

Similar pains are sometimes noted in chronic chloroform takers. ANSTIE thought the latter fact afforded some support to the theory that chloral acts by evolving chloroform in the blood. He expressed the opinion, that some cases of supposed rheumatic or neuralgic pain would be found on careful inquiry to be due to chloral taking, and cited the following case in which this symptom was prominent:

A. B., physician; began the use of chloral February 1, 1873, in 30 grain doses, to procure sleep when kept awake by great anxiety. In two months noticed inflamed and weakened eyes, with scalding tears. Continued the drug, however, sometimes increasing the dose and repeating it. From April to August the usual amount taken was one drachm; in the latter month he commenced using it during the day, one to three times. About December 1st he began to realize the amount he was daily taking, and found it half an ounce, sometimes more. He now began to complain of severe general pains, especially about the joints, which grew worse in the moist air of London; there was no tenderness, and they were not increased by motion. Chloral did not relieve them, except when it put him to sleep. Soon after this he made a mistake in his dose, using from a stronger solution, which brought on the pains with frightful severity, and Dr. ANSTIE was summoned. He found him with suffused eyes, haggard features, sleepless, peculiar, broken speech, partial paraplegia, loss of co-ordination, and excessive joint pains. An examination disclosed that he had taken more than an ounce of chloral the preceeding day. It was at once withdrawn. Cannabis indica was used to relieve the nervous disturbance, tonics given, and under this treatment he recovered.

The following case under our care is of interest:

Mrs. A., age 37; began to suffer from insomnia sixteen years ago, which persisted in varying degree until Dec. 1889, when a severe injury, confining her to bed for fourteen weeks, increased this wakeful condition until it became essential to compel sleep. Chloral secured it. The initial dose was 15 grains, at bed-time. This amount sufficed for 14 months, when she began to suffer severe limb pains—not increased by pressure or movement—which soon resulted in a sharp and prolonged bout of hysteria and nervous prostration with increased agrypnia. The chloral dose was doubled, but without effect. During several weeks various hypnotics were tried, with ill success; her physician declared, "in the endeavor to give her sleep I almost exhausted the Pharmacopœia." Finally hyosciamine was given. This broke the insomnia, but for some reason, after a week's use, recourse was again had to chloral, und this was continued until a week before coming to us, when a new medical advisor decreased it and gave hyoscyamus, with the result of much lessened pain but little better sleep.

At time of placing herself under our care, Mrs. A. was weak, sleepless, anorexic, and greatly depressed; her physician wrote, "this chloral taking, with the shock from the horrible injury she received, has almost entirely wrecked her nervous system." The chloral was at once withdrawn, and 40 grains chloralamid given. It brought a full night's sleep, without ill after-effects. During the following fortnight, various hypnotics, sulfonal, paraldehyde, morphine, codeine, hyoscine, somnal and chloralamid, were used. The last named proved by far the best,—always fetching refreshing slumber for several hours,—and was continued. Meantime she was placed on large doses of strychnine, and two grains thrice daily of quinine. In ten days increased strength permitted a drive, and in a few days more her appearance at every meal. The peculiar pains steadily lessened, and in a fortnight were a thing of the past. The chloralamid was gradually decreased during a month, and then ended. The strychnine and quinine, after a few weeks, were followed by phosphorus and Fowler's solution, with an eight-minute bed-time galvanic seance. Under this treatment Mrs. A. progressively improved in every way, and at this writing she asserts that "life is worth living," and she is "feeling better than for years." To complete and confirm convalescence we have advised, in view of her insomnic record, a sea trip, with a short tour abroad, and the winter spent in Bermuda.

This case is instructive. It proves anew the snareful effect of chloral; yet, despite this and other drawbacks, we consider it, in some form, first among hypnotics. Of all the new claimants for favor in insomnia, the two most effective contain it—somnal and chloralamid. The latter we think the better. While deeming it less likely to enslave by continued use, it certainly is less depressing, and the sequelæ are less unpleasant. We use it largely,— dose, 30 to 60 grains on tongue at bed-time,—and regard it a **very** valuable addition to our resources.

Brooklyn Avenue, Brooklyn, N. Y.

CHLORALAMID IN SURGERY.

By EMORY LANPHEAR, M.A., M.D.
Professor of Orthopaedic Surgery in the University Medical College.

Extract from a Clinical Lecture.

Frequently after an operation of magnitude it is necessary to give the patient something to quiet the nervous system and to produce sleep. It is not always pain which causes restlessness and sleeplessness after the operation—in the majority of cases I am sure that the impression upon the nervous system, and particularly upon the mind, is what leads to the insomnia; for under our antiseptic methods, and especially where the wound has been covered with iodoform—a drug having decided anaesthesic properties— there is but a trifling amount of pain, often none, even after the most severe operative procedures. But as night draws near there is a growing restlessness, and at the hour when sleep should come the patient is anxious, nervous and wakeful. What can be done? The almost universal rule among surgeons is to order a hypodermatic injection of morphine; but I believe this is unjustifiable unless there be some indication for the anodyne effect of the opiate; this is markedly true in abdominal surgery; but in any case-the morphine is objectionable because it is apt to produce vomiting, is certain to seriously interfere with the process of digestion, is sure to induce constipation, and nearly always to give rise to headache, malaise, etc. Chloral has been suggested as a proper hypnotic; but chloral depresses the heart to a dangerous degree, and therefore cannot be used in these cases. Bromides, with hyoscyamus, will sometimes answer the purpose admirably, but most stomachs rebel against this combination, so that it is hardly safe to try it. What then can we use? If a drug can be found which will be free from all these objectionable features it unquestionably will fill an important place in our materia medica.

Such a one, it seems, has been discovered in chloralamid. This comparatively new medicinal agent is prepared by combination of two parts chloral anhydride with one of formamid ; it is found in commerce as a colorless, crystalline substance, nearly tasteless, soluble in about twenty parts of water and two of alcohol. It will keep indefinitely in solution without decomposition, but cannot be dissolved in hot solutions because of chemical changes. It acts very much like chloral and sulphonal, but does not depress the heart like the former, and is much superior to the latter in that it is soluble, exerts no bad influence upon digestion, possesses no diuretic action, never causes pruritus, vertigo, diarrhœa, or other bad symptoms which sometimes follow the administration of sulphonal—in fact, experience is demonstrating the accuracy of REICHMANN's observation: from chloralamid no ill effects in the circulation or in the feelings of patients are to be noted; and, besides, the cost is much less than that of sulphonal. T. LAUDER BRUNTON, in a recent report on the Relative Utility of Different Hypnotics, highly commends it, and states that with reference to certainty of action and the question of tolerance chloralamid surpasses.

It exerts its influence upon both the brain and spinal cord, producing sleep and reducing the motor excitement; it may be regarded as a pure hypnotic without anodyne properties, though some late reports would indicate that it has to some degree the power for partial abolition of pain. It is, then, the ideal sedative, giving prompt and satisfactory action, reliable results and absolute freedom from evil side or after effect.

Its dose is from fifteen to sixty grains. The proper method of exhibition is to give fifteen to thirty grains (according to the condition of the subject), repeating the dose in an hour if the first does not produce sleep; usually from ten to thirty grains give five to eight hours' refreshing slumber. The best method of giving it is to dissolve the required amount in about a tea-spoonful of whiskey or brandy, or in a small glass of wine if the patient prefer. It may also be given in anything containing alcohol in considerable quantities, as tincture cardamom compound, tincture of hyoscyamus, etc. If for any reason it cannot be given in this manner, it may be taken in powder form, and washed down with cold water or cold tea. The direction of W. Hale White, of London, is a good one ; viz., tell the patient to dissolve the powder in brandy, add water to his liking, and drink it shortly before going to bed; this combination with spirits is particularly good in our surgical cases where whiskey is usually indicated, at least in most major operations. If in any case it be better to have the medicine in liquid form, this combination may be prescribed :

R   Chloralamid .... ℥ ij
    Spts. frumenti .... fl. ℥ i
Misce bene ut ft. solut. et adde :
    Syrupum rubi idæi .... fl. ℥ i

Misce. Sig.: Dose, one tablespoonful, to be repeated in one hour if sleep is not produced. This makes a decidedly pleasant mixture of slightly acid taste and fruity aroma and flavor.

Kansas City, Mo.

CARDIAC AFFECTIONS:
CASES IN PRACTICE.—A VALUABLE HYPNOTIC.

By J. Hobart Egbert, A. M., M. D., Ph. D.

Original Communication for Notes on New Remedies.

An available hypnotic (other than opium and its derivatives) that may be administered with safety, and even advantage, in cases of cardiac disease, and following the continued use of which there is little or no reaction, is indeed a desideratum. Of late I have applied the new hypnotic Chloralamid (Schering) to this field with very satisfactory results. The following cases from my note book may prove of interest.

Case I.—Mr. R. P., aged 40, supposed to be troubled with "asthma." General inspection showed patient to be a man of excellent physique. Examination of chest demonstrated lungs to be in good condition, but revealed mitral regurgitation as the cause of the dyspnoea, cough, praecordial distress, etc. Compensating hypertrophy being then insufficient for the general supply of blood demanded by the system, the following was given :

R Spts. Ammon. Aromat............... ℥ i.
  Tinct. Digitalis .... ʒ iv.
  Aqua........................q. s. ad ℥ iv.
M. Sig. ʒ i. t. i. d.

Regulation of diet and very moderate exercise were enjoined. Nervousness and insomnia continuing, the following was added to treatment :

R Chloralamid.................. ...... ʒ iv.
  Spts. Vini Gallici .... ℥ ii.
  Aqua .... ℥ ii.
M. Sig. Tablespoonful (ʒ iv) at bed-time.

Patient progressed nicely under treatment and in due course of time passed from my observation.

CASE II.—Mr. M. P., an alcoholic, with cirrhosis of liver and various complications—among which was fatty heart. Except when under influence of narcotic was highly delirious and made much disturbance. At first employed morphine, but such enormous doses were needed to insure quiet that it was not until decided symptoms of poisoning were present that the desired effect could be obtained. The following was subsequently substituted with very satisfactory results :

R Chloralamid......................... ʒ vi.
  Tinct. Gentian. Co................... ℥ ii.
  Elixir simpl......................... ℥ iii.
M. Sig. ʒ iv. pro re nata.

For heart complication used a pill containing nitroglycerin, strophanthus and belladonna. The progress made by patient was even better than was expected in view of his condition.

CASE III.—"Hyperkinesia Cardiaca"—Miss W., being an exception to the general rule, did not greatly improve under the usual combination for irritable heart, to wit, digitalis and belladonna; but improved rapidly and satisfactorily under following plan of treatment :

R Chloralamid .... ʒ iv.
  Tinct. Belladonnae.................. ʒ ii.
  Elixir simpl...........…q. s. ad........ ℥ iv.
M. Sig. Teaspoonful three times daily—between meals and bedtime.

and R Ferri et quiniae citratis .... ʒ iv.
   Tinct. Nucis Vomicae......... .... ʒ iii.
   Syrup. simpl..........q. s. ad........ ℥ vi.
M. Sig. Teaspoonful after meals.

CASE IV.—One case, in conclusion, in which not only the heart's action was embarrassed, but in which the entire bodily functions were retarded and weakened, and which is of special interest because the condition here reported resulted from, or at least followed, that rare and interesting variety of abortion, viz.: myxomatous degeneration of the chorion villi. The patient (Mrs. W.) having been attended by the writer during this trouble early in the spring, apparently made good recovery and passed from my care. In the fall I was again called to see this patient, who was then said to be "very low." Inquiry revealed the fact that she had been flooding more or less all summer, and although "under treatment" by internal medication had (of course) not been relieved but had become so emaciated and anaemic that I hardly recognized her. The foundation of the trouble was plainly endometretis polyposa. I curetted the cavity of the uterus and subsequently swabbed it with carbolic acid. Owing to the general condition of the patient certain reflex neuroses gave much trouble, the chief of which was an almost intolerable and constant cephalalgia, which was very obstinate but finally yielded to full doses of chloralamid. A convenient dose for similar cases is as follows :

> R   Chloralamid.......................... q. s.
> Spts. Lavandulae Co .... ℥ i.
> Elixir simpl. ....ad.......... ℥ iii. M.

In the further treatment of this case medicated vaginal douches and a course of tonics, with careful attention to diet, were prescribed and a complete recovery was effected.

Besides finding chloralamid useful in other exceptional cases like the above, I have found it to be useful in all varieties of insomnia unaccompanied by pain, and in many cases where pain is present. After its use there is not the subsequent ennui and drowsiness, so frequently observed after the exhibition of sulphonal and allied products. The amount of chloralamid consumed in 24 hours should not ordinarily exceed 120 grains.

Southampton, Mass.

CHLORALAMID IN THE GERMAN PHARMA-COPOEIA.

Chloralamid has been incorporated in the new German Pharmacopoeia,—a most significant recommendation for so new a remedy, discovered and introduced about simultaneously with the completion of the late revision. If we consider the vast number of new remedies of really important value which were not admitted, and the comparatively small number which were adopted, and that of this latter class CHLORALAMID was the most recent, it becomes apparent and self-evident that exceptionally conclusive evidence of the value of CHLORALAMID must have been presented to the Commission, and that this pains-taking examining and deliberative body of experts and scientists gave mature consideration before passing favorably on its admission to the new standard "Arznei-Buch." This action was a most decided triumph for CHLORALAMID, and stands as the highest recommendation and endorsement for the new hypnotic.

THERAPEUTIC VALUE OF CHLORALAMID.

OPINIONS OF PROMINENT PRACTITIONERS.

John Aulde, M. D., Demonstrator of Clinical Medicine, and of Physical Diagnosis in the Medico-Chirurgical College of Philadelphia, Pa.:

"It has the advantage of being readily prepared, and is not objectionable to the palate, while the effect of the drug is manifested within a short time after taking, ranging from one-half to two hours, and fortunately, it continues from six to eight hours. The after-effects, as a rule, are not objectionable."

Louis Bauer, M. D., M. R. C. S. Eng., Prof. of Principles and
   Practice, Clinical and Orthopedic Surgery, Consulting Sur-
   geon to the City and Female Hospitals, Dean of the St. Louis
   College of Physicians and Surgeons, St. Louis, Mo. :

"I have employed chloralamid in several cases of aggravated
insomnia with decided satisfactory results.   The patients were all
of advanced age.   None of them experienced any disagreeable
effects during or following the use of the remedy."

H. G. Brainerd, M. D., Superintendent Los Angeles, Cal., County
   Hospital :

"We have now tried chloralamid with over 30 different patients
and in the majority of the cases were well pleased with the results.
It acts more promptly than sulfonal.   Its effects do not last over
into the next day.   It is more soluble, and hence more easily administered than sulfonal, and it is less expensive."

Daniel M. Brower, M. D. *Medical News,* April 19, 1890 :

"The medical profession to-day is more fortunate than ever
before in the number of sleep-producing remedies.   Sulfonal is a
comparatively recent remedy of great value.   It does not interfere
with the digestion, the circulation, or the heart's action, as chloral,
the bromides, and opium frequently do.   We have also the still
more recent remedy, chloralamid.   It has some advantage over
sulfonal in that it acts more rapidly, and when dissolved in wine
has but little taste.   Sulfonal, on the contrary, probably by reason
of its great insolubility, often acts slowly, its effects being more
manifest the next day than on the evening of its administration.
You can often administer either of these remedies without the patient's knowledge, as they have but little taste."—*Journ. of N. &
M. Desease.*

Dr. George P. Cope, Physician at the Richmond District Lunatic
   Asylum, (*Dublin Journal of Medical Science,* February, 1890),
   describes his experiments with chloralamid, and commends
   the hypnotic without reserve. (See this pamphlet, page 20.)

Chas. F. Folsom, M. D., Co-Referee, Visiting Physician to the
   Boston City Hospital :

"The danger from the large dose, over 30 to 40 grains, is less
than in chloral.   Disagreeable after-effects are much less common.
In my experience, with only the small dose, it has done well."

Dr. Hagen and **Dr. Huefler,** Assistants at the Clinic of Prof.
STRUEMPELL, Erlangen :

"Our experiences—while testing chloralamid—proved so encouraging and apparently so conclusive, that we no longer hesitate,
in view of our experiments, to pronounce it one of the most reliable of hypnotics known to us. *** A comparison between chloralamid and chloral, based on our observations so far, would indicate
preference for the former on account of manifest superiority."

William A. Hammond, M. D., ex-Surgeon General of the U. S.
Army, from his Private Sanitarium at Washington, D. C.,
writes :

"I have used chloralamid in several cases of obstinate insomnia
with excellent results. It appears to be more certain and pleasant
in its effects than any other recently discovered hypnotic." And
again, "I may here state that I have employed chloralamid in other
cases in which sleep was necessary, with great satisfaction."

C. R. Hexamer, M. D., Stamford, Conn. :

"I beg to state that my success with chloralamid has been highly
satisfactory. I have used it since its first introduction, especially
in such cases where formerly I had used chloral. I have used it
with children in gramme doses, considering these equivalent to five
grain doses of chloral; in the cases where used with children, the
age ranged between five and ten years. In two cases of alcoholic
tremor I used chloralamid in from three to four gramme doses with
decided beneficial as well as pleasing effect. I consider three
grammes an average, or ordinary dose, which can safely be given
as the equivalent for 15 grains of chloral. The sleep produced by
chloralamid is in the highest sense refreshing, and from the statements of patients, as well as from my personal experience, three
grammes chloralamid cause a more pleasant sleep with less after-
effect than one gramme chloral."

Frank L. James, M. D., Editor of St. Louis (Mo.) *Medical &
Surgical Journal,* and of the *National Druggist :*

"Since our previous note on the use of chloralamid in insomnia
we have had occasion to test it in two cases of prolonged insomnia,
rebellious to chloral, paraldehyde, etc., and found that it invariably
produced sound and refreshing sleep, without any apparent evil
after-effects. The only sequela noted was a thirst which the pa-

tients experienced shortly after waking, but which was quenched with a glass or two of cold water."

D. F. Kinnier, M. D., New York City:

Report on fifteen cases, in varying degrees of mania, dementia, melancholia and insanity.   Chloralamid, in forty-five grain doses, acted more satisfactorily than sulfonal, bromides or chloral.   Five and six hours sleep were usually secured within 30 minutes to one hour.   The doctor concludes: "In beginning the use of this drug it is preferable to give 25 grains and increase to 45, which dose may be given without any unpleasant symptoms as a rule.   When the chemistry and physiological action of this drug is better understood than it is at present, we may look for better results, and although disappointing in some cases, yet in many cases it will be found a valuable hypnotic."

Dr. Eugen Kny, Ass't Physician at the Clinic for Mental Diseases, University of Strassburg:

"The most important advantage of chloralamid consists of the fact that the drug never affects the circulation, not even during the most profound sleep.   Chloralamid may confidently be recommended as a very powerful, reliable, and harmless hypnotic."

Dr. U. Lettow, Assistant at Clinic, University of Greifswald:

1. Chloralamid is a very useful hypnotic, although it is not absolutely reliable in all cases.

2. It has the preference over other hypnotics because it exerts no influence on the pulse, frequency of respiration or temperature.

3. Collateral symptoms only appear singly, and consist of slight headache and vertigo.

4. The dose in which chloralamid is sure to act in an adult, is 3 grammes.

5. Chloralamid is best given 1 to 1½ hours before bed-time.

6. In the form of an enema, chloralamid is most reliable.

7. Chloralamid in some cases continues to exert hypnotic action far into the day following administration.

Alexander I. Malshin, M. D., house physician to the Prëobrajensky Asylum, Moscow (*Meditzinskoïe Obozrenië*, No. 5, 1890, p. 941);

Describes his experience in regard to chloralamid which he tried

130 times in seventeen cases of various mental and nervous affections. The remedy was given in doses of from 30 to 40 grains, dissolved in water, cold tea or wine. The main outcome of the author's observations may be summarized as follows: 1.—The hypnotic effects of the new remedy are most marked in cases of acute and chronic paranoia, periodic psychosis, neuritis multiplex and subacute articular rheumatism. 2.—Sleep ensues in from one-half to three hours after the ingestion and lasts from two to ten hours. 3.—In cases of mania, progressive paralysis, and paranoia associated with intense exitement, the remedy proves to be either totally ineffective or nearly so. 4.—It should be given dissolved in wine.

A. M. Miller, M. D., Bird-in-Hand, Pa.:

After giving it a trial in a case of insomnia I found it (chloralamid) to excel all other hypnotics that I have ever used. I have since used it with excellent effect, and think chloralamid is one of the best hypnotics we have for the insomnia of old persons and nervous females.

Dr. Conolly Norman, (*Dublin Journal of Medical Science*, January, 1890):

Sulfonal is bulky and practically insoluble, therefore difficult to administer, and, perhaps owing to its insolubility, it is slow in action. The trials with chloralamid were very satisfactory, and we found it not bulky, tolerably soluble, quick in action, thirty minutes to one hour, and now cheaper than sulfonal has ever yet become.

Dr. D. R. Paterson, (London *Lancet*, October 26, 1889):

That this drug will be a valuable addition to our therapeutical armamentarium is undoubted.

Prof. S. Rabow, M. D., Lausanne-Cery:

An entirely new hypnotic which is worthy of consideration in more than one respect, and which will probably find extensive employment in the future. We may already regard the remedy as a worthy addition to our treasure of hypnotics.

Dr. Ed. Reichmann, Medical Clinic of Prof. RIEGEL, Giessen:

Although we still can form no conclusive opinion from what has been said about chloralamid, we may venture to say that the same fulfills all the requirements of a hypnotic.   1.—Safe, prompt action followed doses of 2 to 3 grm., sleep supervening after ½ to ¾ of an hour, sometimes a little earlier, seldom later (just as soon as after sulfonal);   2.—The absence of annoying and under circumstances contra-indicated by-effects,—inasmuch as the patients felt well subjectively upon awaking, and objectively no change in the circulation of the blood was observed.

M. Rosenthal, M. D., resident physician at the Montefiore Home, and visiting physician at the German Dispensary, New York City, contributes a paper to the recent issue of the *Mediçinische Monatsschrift*, detailing and summarizing his very careful and extensive clinical trials with chloralamid. He sums up partly, as follows:

In cases where speedy effect is required chloralamid should be preferred to sulfonal.   In the majority of our cases the patients slept soundly within an hour after taking chloralamid, and many of them sooner.   In patients who are liable to collapse, chloralamid should also receive the preference, as it has no effect on the action of the heart, nor on respiration, while sulfonal frequently produces collapse.

E. C. Rothrock, M. D., Malakoff, Texas:

I have used chloralamid, the new hypnotic, with decided advantage in a number of cases.   Chloralamid is a valuable addition to new remedies.   I prefer it in most cases to opium, sulfonal, hydrate-amyl, or paraldehyde.   The relief which chloralamid affords is attended with less disturbance of the entire system than induced by above remedies or any other drug I have ever used for similar purposes.

S. A. K. Strahan, M. D., Barrister-at-Law and Medical Officer to the County Asylum, Northampton; in the London *Lancet*, Feb. 15, 1890:

Of all the somnifacients discovered of late years I should say that none is likely to prove a more certain sleep producer, and at the same time more innocent and agreeable otherwise, than chloralamid, the last introduced hypnotic. *** It is a very useful and **safe** hypnotic, and may be given to paralytics whatever their stage.

J. M. Thompson, M. D., Boston, Mass.:

I can safely recommend chloralamid in any case where a hypnotic is indicated, and feel sure that it is the best, safest and most reliable in use up to date.

W. V. Whitmore, A. M., M. D., Interne County Hospital, Los Angeles (Cal.):

We have obtained our best results in cases of cardiac asthma and phthisis. The next best results were obtained in cases of organic heart disease, acute alcoholism, pyo-salpinx, hydro-salpinx, hysteria, and in some forms of neuralgia. It has given good results in spinal sclerosis, mania, melancholia, monomania, carcinoma, rheumatism, and typhoid fever.

Even in the cases in which it has been least effective, it still has compared very favorable with the other hypnotics.

It, therefore, seems to have the advantage over *Chloral*:

  1.—It is much more agreeable to the taste.
  2.—It *very* seldom causes digestive disturbances (1% of the cases).
  3.—It does not depress action of the heart or circulation.
  4.—Very rarely does it produce cerebral disturbance (1% of the cases).

Compared with *Sulfonal*:

  1.—It is much more soluble.
  2.—It is more rapid in its action.
  3.—Almost invariably sleep passes away by morning.
  4.—It is less than one-half as expensive.

We desire to give unqualified recommendation to chloralamid. As a hypnotic it is safe, reliable, and efficient. Its side-effects are, almost without exception, valuable additions to it as a remedy. We have yet to learn of any other hypnotic that possesses so many favorable properties and so few unfavorable ones.

ADDITIONAL TESTIMONY FROM AUTHORITIES.

British Medical Association, A special Committee on Therapeutics
   instructed to examine into comparative action of hypnotics,
   reported as follows on Chloralamid:

"In one case twenty grains, and in six cases thirty grains, were
given in single doses.   After the twenty grains, sleep came on in
twenty minutes and lasted three hours with half an hour's interval
of waking; after thirty grains, sleep came on in fifteen minutes to
half an hour (four cases), one to two hours (two cases).   Sleep
lasted all night in three cases, in two cases four and five hours, and
in one case there was two hours dozing, then an interval of wake-
fulness, and then two hours sleep.   No disagreeable after-effects
were observed."—*British Medical Journal*, July 26, 1890.

Dr. Chas. L. Dana, Professsor of Diseases of the Mind and
   Nervous System; Physician to Bellevue Hospital; Neurolo-
   gist to the N. Y. Infant Asylum and the Montefiore Home
   for Chronic Invalids:

Recommends 30 grain doses of Chloralamid ("Neurasthenia,"
in the *Post-Graduate Journal*, Jan. 1891.) for insomnia, as a substitute for bromides after using the latter for a time.

Dr. Umpfenbach, in the Provincial Lunatic Asylum, under the
   direction of Dr. Noetel:

"Chloralamid was given in 55 cases, 23 of which were men and
the remainder women.   It is interesting to learn that in the greater
number of cases the results were everything that could be desired,
although the symptoms in some of the cases were very severe.
Considerable importance must be attached to the observation that
the remedy was well borne in every instance even when taken for
months together; valuable evidence of this was offered by the
body-weight which never decreased during the treatment.
Further, no action on the heart or on the vascular or urogenital
systems could be detected, nor did symptoms of collapse manifest
themselves.   In a single case chloralamid was observed to be
excitant in action, but this only serves to emphasize its advantage
over chloral hydrate which has such an action much more
frequently.   The author concludes that chloralamid must be
regarded as a decidedly useful hypnotic."

Dr. D. S. Moore, Assistant Superintendent at the North Dakota
   Hospital for the Insane, Jamestown, N. D., writes:

"I have used Chloralamid and found it, in cases of insomnia from
habit, restlessness, anxiety, and nervous exhaustion, considering
the ease with which it is administered and its freedom from disagreeable after-effects, the most efficient hypnotic that has come to
my notice."

Dr. Chas. C. Browning, of the New York City Asylum for the Insane, Blackwell's Island, writes:

"In reply to the inquiry regarding the use of Chloralamid in my practice, permit me to say that results have been satisfactory, and I have continued to use it ever since I became acquainted with this new hypnotic."

The Medical Times, New York, writes:

"Chloralamid in Chronic Chorea.—Chronic chorea is now being successfully treated by inducing upon the patient a condition of almost constant sleep for a period of some two weeks, from time to time allowing intervals of consciousness that nourishment may be taken. The hypnotic most recommended is Chloralamid in fifteen grain doses, and repeated sufficiently often to maintain a constant effect.

Dr. J. B. Mattison, member of the American Association for the cure of Inebriates; of the New York Neurological Society; of the Medical Society of the County of Kings, Brooklyn, N. Y., has reported good results with Chloralamid at various times, and in an article on "Hypnal," in the New York *Medical Record*, January 3, 1891, says:

"Following failure (with Hypnal), thirty grains Chloralamid promptly brought slumber. Compared with the latter—which, *en passant*, I think *the* hypnotic—thirty grains hypnal have less power than a like amount of Chloralamid. As an anodyne, sedative, or hypnotic it is less effective than a combination of phenacetine and Chloralamid."

Dr. G. Genersich and Dr. P. Naecke.

"Dr. G. GENERSICH has prescribed Chloralamid in thirty-two cases, giving thirty grains at night. This dose was generally sufficient to induce sleep within half an hour. A more certain effect and a longer sleep was obtained when forty-five or sixty grains were prescribed. He considers Chloralamid preferable to other hypnotics, both because it acts more decidedly and because it is less unpleasant to take. It must be remembered that its effect is negative when sleeplessness is due to pain. It is not by any means a dangerous drug, but headache and vomiting may occur after a very large dose. It does not seem to affect the digestion nor the renal functions. The pulse generally becomes softer and more frequent."—*Med. Record*.

To this we append the communication of our Berlin Correspondent:

"I have had occasion before to refer to the properties of Chloralamid, or chloral formamide. The latest addition to its already copious literature is made by GENERSICH (*Pester med. chir. Presse*) under the title "A contribution to the hypnotic action of Chloralamid." As is so frequently the case with this remedy, his results were favorable and the deduction from his observations may be summed up as confirming the previous statements that

Chloralamid is a decided hypnotic and not a narcotic, that its action is uniform, reliable and free from disturbing secondary manifestations. Sometimes when very large doses are employed slight nausea, headache and giddiness are produced, but these are mild and transient. Further the remedy does not interfere with digestion or affect the kidneys. A dose of 30 grains in the evening, or 45 to 60 grains in the day is sufficient to produce the desired effect; the remedy appears to be specially indicated in the treatment of sleeplessness caused by or dependent upon nervous conditions or affections.

As confirmatory of the conclusions of GENERSICH those of Dr. P. NÆCKE, may be cited. He sums up the indications for the use of Chloralamid as follows:

1. Chloralamid in doses of 15 to 45 grains is a very good and harmless hypnotic for women with chronic mental disease and for epileptics.

2. It produces excellent effect not merely in nervous conditions but also in excitement.

3. In a few cases it has a sedative influence when given at mid-day in doses of 15 to 30 grains.

4. It is best given shortly before the usual time for sleeping.

5. Its effect is more slowly produced and possibly more reliable than that of chloral, at any rate it is less dangerous; Chloralamid induces a lighter but a more refreshing sleep than chloral.

The application of the remedy does not appear to extend to the sleeplessness produced by pain. These results are, however, the more striking as experiments by the same author with hyoscine and amylene hydrate showed that the former is useless, while the latter sometimes produces great depression and when given in epilepsy may increase the number of attacks."

Dr. Chas. E. Denhard, member Academy of Medicine, Medico-Legal Society, N. Y. Medical Union, Med. Chirurg. Society of German Physicians, etc., New York City: informs us that he has had most excellent results from 30 grain doses of Chloralamid in cases of painful menstruation in young women, where the administration of various opiates had to be excluded for fear of inducing habitual use of same. Dr. DENHARD'S suggestion has the merit of originality, and, we are glad to state, has been privately circulated and adopted by many physicians with family practice. It is a valuable recommendation for Chloralamid to know that a thirty grain dose, administered as the painful period approaches, will induce quiet slumber and furnish perfect relief before re-awakening; it is also proof that Chloralamid is possessed of some analgesic action. Dr. DENHARD reports further that he is using Chloralamid regularly in his practice wherever a hypnotic is indicated, and that he successfully applied it recently in an aggravated case of neurasthenia, affording patient, a young girl of 18 years, unwonted relief.